A Shape of My Own

A Shape of My Own

GRACE BOWMAN

VIKING
an imprint of
PENGUIN BOOKS

VIKING

Published by the Penguin Group

Penguin Books Ltd, 80 Strand, London WC2R ORL, England

Penguin Group (USA) Inc., 375 Hudson Street, New York, New York 10014, USA

Penguin Group (Canada), 90 Eglinton Avenue East, Suite 700, Toronto, Ontario, Canada M4P 2Y3
(a division of Pearson Penguin Canada Inc.)

Penguin Ireland, 25 St Stephen's Green, Dublin 2, Ireland (a division of Penguin Books Ltd)

Penguin Group (Australia), 250 Camberwell Road,
Camberwell, Victoria 3124, Australia (a division of Pearson Australia Group Pty Ltd)

Penguin Books India Pvt Ltd, 11 Community Centre,
Panchsheel Park, New Delhi – 110 017, India

Penguin Group (NZ), cnr Airborne and Rosedale Roads, Albany,
Auckland 1310, New Zealand (a division of Pearson New Zealand Ltd)

Penguin Books (South Africa) (Pty) Ltd, 24 Sturdee Avenue,
Rosebank, Johannesburg 2196, South Africa

Penguin Books Ltd, Registered Offices: 80 Strand, London WC2R ORL, England

www.penguin.com

First published 2006

I

Set in Monotype Bembo 12/14.75pt
Typeset by Palimpsest Book Production Limited, Polmont, Stirlingshire
Printed in Great Britain by Clays Ltd, St Ives plc

A CIP catalogue record for this book is available from the British Library

ISBN-13: 978-0-670-91618-4
ISBN-10: 0-670-91618-8

For Linda

Contents

Acknowledgements

This book wouldn't have come to life without Liz Attenborough's encouragement and belief in me: thank you for everything.

Many thanks to Tony Lacey and Zelda Turner for giving me a first opportunity to share my words and for seeing something important in them.

Nothing would be possible without my amazing family and friends who love and support me always and no matter what; this is for you all.

And finally to Max. Thank you for helping me to give this story a happy ending.

Edges and Centres

If I share a secret with you, do you promise to tell everyone?

This is not a secret to be kept inside any more. This is not a secret to be shrouded and embedded in hushes and quietness. This secret will not be one that forges itself into deep wrinkles and is held fast with a sharp intake of breath. This is a story to be told. It is a story to be shared, and shared out loud, to be discussed and considered and passed on.

Pass it on.

It is a story which I feel I need to tell. At the moment, it is only in my head – almost as if it didn't happen. I don't speak about it any more. Some people know fragments, but no one has heard the whole thing from beginning to end, although these two folds of my tale are hard to define. I struggle with where to start.

I could explode my narrative with a bold statement: 'One day I wake up and I'm an anorexic.'

But that's not really true, so I could start: 'One day I wake up and someone tells me that I'm an anorexic. So before, things are fine, I'm just me, and the next day, someone gives me a label, which makes me someone completely different. One day you know me, the next day I'm a presence you hardly recognize.'

I could even contextualize it: 'I was eighteen when I was labelled anorexic. I was caught up in getting through being a teenager, I was spun out, tongue-tied, I felt displaced, disrupted. I was changing, and anorexia did change me.'

Or, I could take you back to my beginnings. I would start with those pre-memories; the parts of me before the eating disorder took hold. I could say, 'My tale begins with my childhood. I grew up in my semi-detached house on a north-eastern street with my two sisters and my brother and my mum and my dad. My house had a back and front garden and I had a little bedroom with my books and my toys. I was happy and stable. I was what people might term "normal". At my primary school and my comprehensive school I wore the same uniform as everybody else. I did my homework, I liked boys who didn't like me back, I had friends; I grew like everybody else did.'

It is hard to locate the right memories for a beginning: to decide which ones are relevant to the overall picture. We always take ourselves back to the start to try and find out why things happened; to try and force some blame into some day or some month or into some half-shaded memory. I don't find my experience as simple an equation as that. I suppose this is because I have relatively few strong child-hood imprints. I cannot put those years on to a film in my head – rerun even a day as if I were living it. I only have blank snapshots, hardly seen through my eyes at all – unin-habitable frames. Thumbing through photo albums I see pictures that show I once smiled and tell me that I existed, but if you took them away, I wonder if I would remember anything much at all. There are flashes of childhood memo-ries, which add themselves into my story, but when I look at the whole they don't stand out. These are the days of childhood that are blended, or lost, or forgotten about, where the seams of my memory are almost too perfect to be able to dissect and pull apart. There will be times, distinct and clear to others, things that I said (or didn't say), which they hold firmly in their minds, but which I have stopped up, never to explore again because I didn't think them significant, or because they have simply slipped away. In this way, I suppose that my narrative will be incomplete because it cannot tell everything. But in its making it will reveal how I remember: how I build my identity and my history from a handful of images, which shape my understanding of myself as a child, and which I use to try and interpret my adult self; the whys and wherefores of me, now. I could tell you about such memories and you could forge an understanding of me; perhaps it would help.

'I am on the beach with my bucket and spade by the frosty North Sea. I am squatting by the edge of the shoreline and smiling at the camera, with sand in my hands and grains falling through the cracks between my tiny fingers.' But the reality is that I can't remember that sand, that frost, that day, that year. My childhood memory has been fostered by others, those who lived it with me, who brought me up and who have replayed parts of it back to me. And now as I recount it, years will become paragraphs, ages turn to simple numbers and then all of a sudden childhood is over and there are new beginnings on the horizon.

Perhaps, then, I should begin my secret story with an ending, an ending that would explain to you that I have moved beyond this experience and that, 'Now, after the event, I am something different again. This is a story of recovery and hope. There is a me beyond the thin, absent person reflected in the dictionary definition: "*Anorexia nervosa: absence of appetite of a nervous origin*".'

This is a definition, anyway, which no one seems to properly understand. A term which obfuscates and closes up something that thrives and survives upon the secrecy it is afforded. This should not be an account of absence and of whispers. It is a story of the presence of something, which strangles and takes hold and manipulates. It is also about finding a centre, and discovering a shape.

This story will also reflect the shape of many people's lives. As someone with an eating disorder in the UK, I was not one in a million. I was not one in a thousand. I was not one in a hundred. It may be that I was as many as one in sixty.[1] It could well be more. And what I experienced may be a part of everyone in some way or another.

If I was so different, strange and alien, then I might find my experience harder to admit – I might find it difficult to present myself in this way – but I know that I am not. It is only because more people have not spoken up about this that it seems like I am telling something extraordinary, something at the edge of our lives and not at the centre.

The theories on anorexia nervosa pile on top of one another; they do not make sense. They contradict and argue over causes and issues and blame. This public fight over our bodies ends up marginalizing many and compartmentalizing others. No wonder the illness did not make sense to me at the time, nor is it clear to many others now. Indeed, through the passage of my experience, I came to lose all understanding of my own centre and my own edges. So people moved me out of *their* centre of things and on to the periphery, because I did not make sense to them either. Telling this story now, I might start to move those boundaries and judgements; that is my hope.

So, I have this story to share and in its telling I break a secret code. In putting down my story into words, I even risk the reinforcement of the messages within that code. I risk that some of those still living inside anorexia, without clear perception, will read messages in my text. Strange as it may sound, it might lead them to try and imitate, even emulate, my behaviour, twisting it to their own needs. But, as with any code – one that appears mysterious from the outside – it needs to be broken to allow those from beyond its boundaries to understand it. Without understanding, it remains cloaked in myth, and people like me will continue to feel that it is best to be hushed about their lives. And all of this closure will not help the people trapped within the rules of anorexia to get out of it. Nor will it help those on the outside, families and friends and helpless onlookers, to get under the skin of this illness. I want to share my experience with you to shatter the mystery, to take away the clouds of shame attached to it and to talk about it right from the inside as well as the out.

I want to bring this story together. I want to make sense of it. I want to reinhabit it, so that it no longer remains a separate part of me, but one that contributed to me, in the present, to the shape that I am now, and to the shape of the world around me.

PART I

A View from the Outside

One

The growing-up house was perched on the slope of the hill, facing open landscapes which stretched to Grace's child's eye like squares on her drawing paper, plots in the distance, marking out unvisited areas, new imaginings. She sensed the edges of her world as the edges of this quiet, loving space. Her quietness was undisturbed until the birth of her siblings, when textures and colours previously unseen appeared and showed her new possibility. The little house on the hill squeezed in its occupants, sheltering them from the outside, wombing them in its warmth. And as the family grew, more bricks were added and a coat of paint was splashed on the protective walls; an old carpet stretched to fit the growing spaces. The house moved and pulsed and breathed more heavily as each body got bigger within it.

Three: Grace is taken up the snow-covered hill by Mum who pushes the buggy to and from the small, motionless town. Some days they take the bus; Mum smiles down on her daughter, as they wait in the bus station where north-east accents echo in the dampness. The rain drips down the hood of Grace's shiny red waterproof mac, along the folds of her eyelids and glides off the edge of her cold nose.

Baby brother's arrival confuses Grace's own sense of specialness, and she sulks with her dark brown ringlets in the corner of the room. Mum and Dad divide up the bedroom with a partition wall, taking over her space for him, with his ringing cries and broad blue eyes. She feels unsure of this new arrival in her perfect little world. He is fed and he is nurtured, and it seems to her that he has no judgements or expectations placed upon him. His delicate fair hair is gentle and light. His lightness matches his mum's own. Grace watches him closely. He has taken the attention and focus away from her.

Five: Grace goes to school. She is the first, ahead of the little brother. Gold stars, happy faces, ticks, well done! She is invited to lots of other children's houses, which do not feel quite like her own warming one.

'Would Grace like to come round and play?' one mum says.

'I'm sure she would love to. Would you like to?' Mum tilts her head and smiles. Grace is not sure and scowls back at Mum. She hides behind Mum's long maroon skirt and nods reluctantly.

Dad takes her to the door. They knock. Another dad answers. Grace starts to cry. She screams; she cannot go in, she is terrified: 'Daddy, don't make me go.'

Daddy shouts loudly at her in the middle of the street. She doesn't like it when he shouts because he never usually does. Not at all. But she knows there is always a way out, she should never have to do anything she doesn't want to – Mummy and Daddy will protect her.

Mum comes out of the hospital, opens the car door and sits down slowly. Grace jumps up and down on the back seat. Mum is going to have twin babies. Mum and Dad look worried because, even though it is the best, amazing day, life is going to be too expensive with four children. Dad feels sick and can't eat his fish and chips – they go cold. Grace is happy, though, because it means that she will be special and everyone at school will want to know about the little twin babies. Gold stars, full marks, happy faces.

Six: Dad walks in the door. 'It's twin girls. You are the big sister of lovely baby twin girls!'

Gran picks her up and swings her around and around, and Grace laughs. 'Can we have twin boys next week?' little brother protests.

Grace tuts at his silliness.

Eight: The happy-filled, children-filled growing-up house is busy now. There are crying babies and there is a tired mummy. Grace sees Mummy cry and doesn't like it.

Grace likes to watch over her little sisters to help Mummy out. They are perfect and soft and gentle and cuddly. She looks at them in their cots and wants them to wake up so she can play with them. She feeds them in their side-by-side high chairs. She makes them fish fingers and beans and puts the plastic spoons into their little mouths and they throw it all back into their red plastic bibs.

In Grace's family, there is control. Orange squash is full of sugar and is not good for you. Coke isn't allowed because it costs too much money and runs out quickly.

Grace goes to the supermarket with Dad to help him with the shopping. Grace leads the way. She knows a lot. She licks her lips over Lemon Barley Water: 'Please, Daddy.'

But Daddy says no. Mum and Dad can't believe that anyone would feed children with such sugariness. One of Mum's friends gives her little baby Cadbury's Buttons – Mum's mouth drops open.

Nine: Grace is scared of dogs and roller coasters and most animals and strange places – lots of things. She is an expert at running away, faking illness to escape things that she would not like to do, not in a million years, like going to the dentist or competing in a drama competition, or going for a walk with dogs (even if they are on leads and 'would never hurt anybody'). The fear grabs her in the tummy and so she stays in her room and hides in her wardrobe and makes up stories, much more exciting than any ride in a fun fair, anyway.

Grace likes to be the top girl.

'Test me, Mummy, test me on these questions,' Grace asks.

'Dad, let's go through a list of all the capitals of all the countries of the world – me first!'

'OK, if that's what you want, bubs.' Dad smiles.

Grace must always be the first person to finish her work at school. She makes sure that she gives a loud sigh as she turns over the final page of her mental arithmetic test and glances up at the other girls who speed against her, just to let them know that she is winning. Grace races to be at the top. She makes some little mistakes but she doesn't care because as long as she is in the lead then people talk about her. That is what she likes – people to know how good she is. It gives her a buzzy feeling when she is the best.

Janet and John has been replaced with some new modern books and Grace is on a high level. Not the top level, though. She is annoyed about that. The teacher obviously hasn't thought it through properly. If Miss knew her better then things would be different. She is not a very good teacher if she doesn't think about Grace's ability enough. Gold stars, top marks, happy faces. Tick, tick, tick.

Ten: Grace makes up plays and always takes the main part: Juliet, Audrey Hepburn, Cinderella. Sometimes in the proper school plays the teachers make her the understudy or the second lead. What do they know? It makes her hurt and cry. They prefer another pretty girl. Secretly, Grace is so jealous that she wants to tear her own hair out. It makes her feel sick that someone else has got her part, and the applause and attention with it. She is happy when it turns out that girl can't sing too well.

Grace writes a story about a successful racing driver who is a girl. 'Formula One Girl' wins the race and beats all the boys. The moral of the story is that girls are better than boys. Girls had not been allowed to work and make money and be a success, not in the olden days. Grace would like to be successful when she is grown up. Grace is sure that Mum would be happy about that because she is a feminist.

'I've decided to start my own business. Smash Fashion. I've designed some clothes, and I'm going to make them and then sell them. I'm going to be a fashion designer.'

Grace holds a coffee morning with her best friend in her big garden to raise money to buy the material to make clothes, but the other Durham mums complain. 'It's not ethical for ten-year-old children to keep money from this kind of thing, they must give it to charity.'

Grace runs up to her friend's bedroom and cries. 'It's my Smash Fashion and it's my money.'

She sits on her second-hand bike and longs to ride away – ride away from the mums and the friends and the school and the small city, and realize her big plans.

Eleven: Grace sits on the concrete steps of her new school. She is surrounded by nervous-looking girls and boys in grey and black uniform. She is glad that the teacher tells the class that they have to, 'sit with somebody that you don't know'.

Grace doesn't have anybody she wants to sit with, anyway. Her best friend from junior school has found somebody else to be friends with.

The form teacher pulls her aside. Grace tells the teacher that she isn't happy and that she doesn't have any friends, not at this big school. The girls in her class have called her a flirt. She was reading the boys' palms. One girl pulls her tie, and pulls her hair, and calls her posh. She is not posh. Don't they all know where her mum and dad come from?

'It's because they're jealous,' Mum says.

Jealous of what? Grace thinks.

How can she be popular? What can she do to make them like her? There must be something she can do to get them to talk to her. There are a couple of girls she is obsessed with. The pretty ones who stand out, who seem like they are always surrounded by the most popular people and who smoke on the school bus and go out and rebel. She stares at them, completely transfixed. She knows where they live and what they wear and they probably don't even know her name. She would do anything to be like them. Just anything. Everything would be OK if they accepted her. She hears about their adventures – drinking at the weekends, getting their stomachs pumped, going to concerts, hanging out with boys from the year above. She harbours her desires secretly, folds them inside her tummy, away from everything.

Thirteen: Grace sits at her wooden, stale varnish-smelling desk in a boring geography lesson. The teacher is talking about the movement and collision of tectonic plates. Grace is thinking about the nature of time, and how she can't seem to get a grasp on it. She repeats to herself over and over in her head, 'Remember this moment, no, remember this moment, no, this moment.'

She feels like time is pulsing beneath her and inside her and yet she can't understand how it works. She can't seem to find herself in the present; she is always ahead of it. She is not speaking or acting or even thinking in it. She can't understand it; it makes no sense.

Fourteen: Grace is always the last girl in the line to be picked when the class has to play games in PE lessons. She doesn't really care because she doesn't like things like that. She is not good at sport. She doesn't much see the point of it either. She is not interested in running or physical body activities. And she certainly doesn't want to win at something she can't do properly.

Food is a practicality; eating is simply something you do every day. Grace never really thinks about it. Occasionally, when friends talk about their weight, she thinks about how she has grown a bit, that she is no longer the shape that she used to be. But change has been quite exciting: there was a classroom competition of armpit hair, then a race to start your period, watching each other's growing breasts to guess who might have started early.

As Grace catches up with some of the early developers she feels such pride as she stands in the bathroom after school on her fourteenth birthday and her period finally arrives. She wants to tell all her friends, let them know, but she decides not to and feels a special power in her secret achievement.

Grace's new Best Friend has had her periods for years. She is way ahead of the rest of the girls in all respects. She is the cleverest person. She writes essays and they are read out in front of the class. It's really hard to catch up with her. Things at the big comprehensive are much more complicated. Grace has to push, push, push to try and compete with Best Friend and she struggles. Best Friend is busy dieting and wearing red lipstick and short black dresses, while Grace is still grappling with how to use a tampon. Best Friend is always dieting. She has one bar of chocolate and a Diet Coke for her lunch and she never eats breakfast. At least, that is what she says. Grace tries it; she eats a bread roll for lunch with no butter, nothing else. It feels strange

– the emptiness in her stomach – but she is not sure what it means. She stands outside the classroom, ready for the lesson after lunch. She wants to tell people how she hasn't eaten anything much, but for some reason it feels better to keep it inside.

Best Friend tells Grace that she sometimes faints because she doesn't eat. Grace doesn't get it. Best Friend is always crying and angry. Grace doesn't think it makes sense. Why wouldn't she just eat some more? Grace doesn't really think about diets or food or anything like that.

Grace goes to Best Friend's house and Best Friend buys her a chip buttie. Grace is full so she decides not to eat it all. Best Friend storms into a rage and tells Grace that she is a really bad person.

'Think of all the people in Ethiopia!'

Best Friend doesn't speak to Grace for the rest of the night. Grace sits on the bed and reads magazines and waits to be spoken to. She goes over and over things in her head but daren't talk to Best Friend about any of them. She doesn't like confrontation or angry voices. All she wants is for people to like her, and she will do just about anything for that.

Fifteen: Grace doesn't like the fighting and the dieting and the intensity of things with Best Friend. So she decides to make friends with a group of girls who go out into town on Friday nights. They sit by the river and drink plastic bottles of strong, sweet cider. They dance and dance and drink and drink. It is what she has always wanted to do. She is even hanging out in the same places as the girls she used to stare at, and they actually speak to her! She stands, with her dyed black hair, in her black DM boots, which she has decorated with Tippex, her blue vintage velvet jacket and she pulls at her short skirt. She watches the world spin around her as she stands at the back of the rowing club on the river and lets a boy find his way up her top. The kissing is full and intrusive. She can hardly breathe as he takes over her mouth. She imagines telling people about her latest kissing story. Her head floats away.

Her growth halts – she is shaped. Her fat cells are ready to shift and move into this new body. She is small and has small curves. The excitement fades. She doesn't think about whether she likes her body. She dresses it to fit in, and allows boys to explore what she hasn't even begun to discover herself. One by one they encroach upon her space and she smiles, laughing at her rebelliousness, without considering if she likes it.

'I'm not sure,' she stutters.

Sixteen: Grace is nice and controlled. Things are organized and ordered and she keeps everything to time. She always does her homework and she doesn't get distracted. When she says she is getting up to do something, then she is getting up to do it. Nothing gets in her way. Success is everything. She likes to arrange things, and people. Some of her friends come round and play with her little brother and sisters. They do headstands on the carpet in the living room and play *Guess Who?* Grace thinks that they are terribly immature. They make her angry. Can't they be serious, just for a few minutes? Grace does well in her GCSEs. All As and A*s. She is acknowledged. She has achieved. It must continue.

Grace goes out with one of the most popular boys in the year. She stands in the playground and imagines the teachers looking at her and thinking, 'What is a nice girl like that doing with a boy like him?'

She is pleased by the show they have put on. They must be talking about her now.

Seventeen: An older boy who actually has a car drives Grace home from school. She hopes that someone will spot her and think that she is cool, or better than they perceived. He asks her, 'What kind of music do you like?'

And she thinks to herself, *What answer does he want me to give him? What kind of music does he like?* She scrambles through her head to think of something correct and impressive to say, and instead she replies, 'Oh, you know, everything really. What do you like?'

And then she feels useless, and can't even listen to his response, because she is thinking, *INXS, INXS, that's who I like.*

Eighteen: Grace's eighteenth birthday is the best birthday ever. She drinks champagne with Mum and Dad in the morning and when she gets to school her friends have set up a birthday banner and a table of presents in the sixth-form area. After school Grace has a special takeaway pizza for tea, then she goes to the pub in the evening and orders her first officially allowed alcoholic drink. She is pleased that she is one of the first in the year to turn eighteen, she prefers it that way – being older, being first.

There is change. All of a sudden people are talking about university applications, the end of school and moving away. The stability of family and surroundings are about to become a part of the past. She is going to have to move on – go it alone. She struggles to imagine this new position; she curls up, digging her nails into her forehead and searching for a reply to tell herself it will be all right. She finds none; it is too intangible. She tries to imagine a place, a room, a lecture, something to make this space of university into something she can hold on to. She lies in bed, alone and crying. It is dark, and the world is asleep. She feels the fuzz of tiredness, and can no longer tell if she has already fallen asleep or has been conscious the whole time. She feels the grip of illness, a thumping headache, a sore throat; she holds her breath.

The doctors take a while to find out what is wrong. But when they tell her, she feels relieved because there is something real – something she can feel and explain – she has got glandular fever. Everyone is very sympathetic. She has a lot of time alone, lying down, watching endless daytime TV, and starts to feel differently about herself. She is not hungry and her throat is too sore to swallow so she can only eat half a piece of toast a day. The days are long and empty. Her head spins with thoughts.

I can't do my work. I'm going to get behind. This is my final year of school. I need to get the best marks. I can maybe even get all As. I can, if I try. But not if I'm ill, lying here. I might fail.

She lies on the sofa. Mum strokes her head and soothes her and everything feels a bit better. She senses an isolation she has never experienced before, and she quite likes the peace. A friend comes round and puts some music on – loud on the hi-fi. Grace wants her to leave, she needs her own space and the friend is getting in the way of her carefully organized routine.

It is strange when she goes back into school six weeks later. She decides to pick up some notes, so she can catch up with the lessons she has missed. It feels like her first day all over again. Her head of year meets her in the corridor. She tells him that she is feeling better, but she is shaking, her legs are shaking after the three-minute walk up the hill from her house. He tells her to go home and get better before coming back. The corridors are empty; everyone is in lessons. She thought it would be better that way, so that she wouldn't have to see anyone. Then, all of a sudden, it is break time and people stream towards her; it is noisy and bustling. She feels the tremor of panic. They all carried on

as normal without her, but things don't feel normal now.
She goes home and cries. Home feels small and claustrophobic, after six weeks on the sofa in the silence of the
chatter of daytime TV.

Grace goes to a party and feels a bit left out. She has changed.
    'You've lost weight, Grace,' one girl remarks.
    Grace has never really been told that before, it hasn't been
a point of interest. But she sees the light in the girl's eye
and it feels like a real compliment.

Back at school a second time and it is mock A-level exams.
Grace is quite often the best girl in the class. She smiles as
the teachers hand back her marked exam papers, and they
smile at her. The top girl. Top marks. Best. They say to her,
'You can do it, easy.' 'We know that you'll succeed.'
    It is a bit embarrassing always being at the top. Grace
sometimes thinks that she would rather be a bit more like
the other girls, so as not to be envied or marked out for her
difference. She covers her success as much as she can, and
bows her head so that no one thinks she is being arrogant.
No one likes a clever girl, not really, and especially not one
who people describe as pretty, too. The labels feel wrong.
It means that she is constantly judged.
    'It's only her make-up.'
    'Her figure isn't that nice.'
    She pretends that it is paranoia, that they aren't staring
and commenting, but she feels the heat on her forehead and
a sudden consciousness of the movement of her feet, trailing
behind her, as she head-down-walks across the sixth-form
room carpet.
    Succeed. Success. Succeed. Get away from the judges.
Leave it behind.

★

What if I am poorly and alone and hurting and there is no one to hold my hand and look after me? I want my mum and dad to tell me it's all right. I am hurting and aching all over and I need my mum. I don't want to go to university. I don't want to go away.

She eventually drifts into sleep. She is not as strong as you think. She is not the leader you thought she was. She has skipped childhood to win the race, and now she feels more like a child than ever.

Two

Grace looks at herself in the reflection of the glass-paned double doors between the kitchen and the playroom of her growing-up house. In the reflection she can see her new pinstripe trousers, which she bought on a shopping spree for her eighteenth birthday. The material is thick, rough and wintry and it itches at her skin. The trousers taper in at the bottom, and with them, she wears some silver shoes, which have a big chunky heel. She bought them for school, for the sixth form, because sixth form means fewer rules, and you are allowed to wear heels of some sort. Grace doesn't like the rules because there is always the fear that she might break one, and that isn't something she wants to do.

'Get your blazer back on,' the teachers shout at her. 'Take that lipstick off.' She shudders inside, but smiles on the outside, because it is not a good thing to show that you are affected or worried by being told off, but she is, deeply.

After years of wishing for it, being eighteen is strange. Everyone around her makes it into a big deal, a defining moment. Grace is no longer growing up, but a 'grown-up' – able to do things and firmly in control.

In the thick glass reflection, Grace can see her smart outfit. She is ready to go out to town. She is dressed up, make-up layered thick. She is wearing a gold-coloured polo-neck jumper with short sleeves, which is made of a stretchy sort of material. Grace plays with it; she stretches the sleeves about, pulling them down her arms. She lifts her foot off the floor and brings her knee up so that she is standing on one leg and looking at the other one in the glass. She stops.

She tilts her head. She looks at the thick material at the top of her trousers, which is bunching up, and she observes the shape of small rolls of flesh at the top of her thigh, squashing beneath the fabric. She looks again into the thick glass of the double doors. Her image is criss-crossed by the wood framing and she says out loud, 'Do you think I need to lose some weight?'

She shows Mum the tight trousers. Mum gives a semi-smile. 'Oh love, you don't need to. Aren't you funny!'

Grace goes out for the evening and she has some drinks with her friends, laughing, joking; having fun. She eats some chips as she stands in the market place in the long queue and waits for a taxi home with all the drunken people, and she says goodbye to her friends and she comes home, just like normal.

Wolf whistles from the builders in the car park. Mr Driving Examiner smirks. 'Someone is popular, aren't they?'

Grace feigns a smile and pulls down her smart black skirt to cover more of her legs, which are semi-masked under her black tights. They drive. Grace completes the manoeuvres. Success. Succeed. Finish.

Get it right, Grace. Get it right. Got to pass first time to make it. Got to be the best. Pass the driving test and get back to revision. A levels. Everything is dependent on these results. There is no chance of a failure. It is just not possible. Get it right, Grace. Come on. Get it right.

'So, what are you going to do at university?' Mr Driving Examiner turns his head.

'Sorry?' Grace isn't prepared for him to actually speak to her.

'At university, what are you going to study?' Mr Driving Examiner repeats as he relaxes back into his seat.

'Drama,' Grace tells him. 'I want to be an actress.'

'Very nice.' Mr Driving Examiner smiles. 'So are you going to be like Sharon Stone in that film?'

Grace giggles nervously. Unsure what to do with the wolf whistles and the flirtatious comments.

She gets full marks on the over-prepared Highway Code, recited and recited to perfect precision.

'I am pleased to say that you have passed your driving test.'

Grace takes the piece of paper from Mr Driving Examiner and counts up the number of minor errors she made (she definitely does not like errors, mistakes, failures – however they want to phrase it). She will not reveal that information to anyone, thank you very much.

She goes home and runs down the drive waving the Pass piece of paper in her hands. Another thing achieved. Smiling faces at her first-time success and best of all, no failure – an impossible consideration.

Grace sits in the driving seat, with her boyfriend beside her, in Dad's car. It feels wrong.

'I'm scared.'

Boyfriend laughs.

'I don't think I can do it. I don't remember what to do. I keep having these dreams about the car going out of control. The brakes won't work. I can't get into the parking spaces. I can't make that kind of a judgement. What if I get it wrong? What if I make a mistake and I crash or I hit someone's car? I couldn't handle it. I can see it happening in my head. People are hooting their horns, shouting at me, and I'm just sitting there, not even remembering which pedal is which.'

'I thought you wanted to drive. Do you want me to?' Boyfriend asks.

'I'll be fine. I'll be OK. I've just got to do it.'

Grace starts the car. Her foot is vibrating, her whole leg is shaking, all the way up to the top. She starts to drive, hesitantly, tensed-up and terrified of making a mistake.

Got to keep driving, Grace. Just forget the fears. Eating you up, aren't they? Feel like a failure for the deep white scratch you made on the side of the red car. Misjudged the width, backing into the drive, didn't you? Can't do anything, can you? No good. Not even after all those months of lessons and practice. Hear that screech of the side of the car against the concrete wall. Ouch. Hear it over and over again.

Things seem strange, don't they? Not quite right. This is the one chance you have to shape the future. Everything is changeable, on the edge. Have a daydream. Go on. Sit and think of something. Something to help make things better, more bearable.

Got to do well. Got to get top marks. Got to be pretty. Got to have best friends. Got to be popular. Got to go to the best university. Got to be the best in class. Got to keep the boyfriend.

'You'll be fine.'

'You always do well.'

'It can't be difficult for you!'

'We know you're the best.'

The voices of everyone around her are played back loud.

Got to be thin! If only I were thin. That's it. That's what can be changed. Got to be thinner.

Three

Grace runs down the stairs to the letter box. She knows that the post will bring news of rejection or acceptance from her chosen universities, delivered to the door. She opens the envelope; it is the third one to arrive and the first rejection. She doesn't know what to do with rejection. She throws the letter in the bin. She decides to keep the news inside, pretending that it didn't happen. She sits on the secret all morning. At lunchtime, over bread rolls and milk (cheap school dinners to save money for pints of cider on Friday night), she tells her friends.

'I didn't want to go there, anyway,' she preempts them.

They look surprised, thinking about how she always does well, always seems to find things easy.

'Sorry,' they say.

I hate the word sorry. I haven't really failed. Let's get back to you. Let's not dwell on me. It wasn't right, anyway. I never wanted to go there. Never, not one bit. Don't look at me like that. Don't be sorry.

Grace comes home from school; she takes off her uniform and changes into her smart outfit with her high-heeled boots, just so that she looks acceptable in case anyone should see her. She applies her make-up, and sits in her bedroom waiting for her boyfriend to come over. He doesn't arrive. He doesn't call. He forgets to send her a Valentine's card. He isn't going to university; he certainly isn't coming with her. Things are changing.

Grace doesn't have a problem with self-discipline, not like Boyfriend does. She does what is needed, and she does it all on time. She doesn't hand her homework in late. All under control. Nice and controlled. All in order. It is just irritating that Boyfriend keeps getting in the way. She doesn't like the way she is always thinking of him. He is annoying now, taking up too much of her revision time and spoiling all the perfect plans.

Dad helps her revise. Grace wants to do well in her A levels. What Grace wants, Grace gets. She wants to be one of the people whose name makes it on to the school news-letter – an A4-photocopied piece of paper with the school logo on it. If she gets all A grades then she will be recognized on there. She did it for her GCSEs – she was acknowledged. She keeps that newsletter in a box in her wardrobe with certificates, badges and other assorted items that show her that she has done well. Grace paces up and down the house, up and down, up and down, reciting bits of history, French verbs, literary quotes. She draws up a detailed plan and sticks it on the wall over her bed. She rewrites all of her notes on to neat and lined pieces of paper. She asks Dad to test her.

'OK, Grace, tell me about Lord Liverpool,' Dad says.

She sees the words from the page in her mind, she holds them all in her head; she has a very good memory for facts. She tells him about Lord Liverpool and then she carries on. She takes him through Wellington, Peel and Palmerston to Disraeli, Gladstone and beyond. Not a detail missed. Dad silently turns page after page. He smiles at her. He says nothing. He never has to say anything. Grace is a good daughter, who he is sure will do well in her A levels, like she has done well in everything else. So different from his own experience of school. He is proud of her, how she has moved on from where he was.

Grace sits on the floor and looks at the Easter eggs in front of her. One by one she puts them to her side, then she gets up, sits on the sofa and looks down on them. She is too old for Easter eggs, anyway; they are something for her little brother and sisters, something for childhood, not grown-up Grace. If she gives them to her little brother and sisters, then they will be happy and she will be healthier. No big deal.

She stepped on the scales and was heavier than she thought (she was heading for nasty nine stone), and it didn't feel nice, so she is cutting down on food. Since glandular fever knocked her down and then she got 'all better' again, she has put on a bit of weight. Nobody has mentioned it, but surely they must see it . . . surely? They must be able to see what she can clearly feel. So it is a diet. It is not something that will be shouted about, but it is a good thing and it will help her feel better. She will be more prepared for her exams and clearer about university. She will simply look better if she weighs a little less – a new image for a new place.

Grace has been up and down the country looking at universities. Mostly they are in the south of England, miles away from home.

Who would want to stay here?

She must get these exams right to make sure that she can get away. She goes to Bristol and stays with a friend's sister in a student flat. They eat spaghetti bolognese together, and Grace tries to think of some interesting things to say. There is a coldy feeling inside her in this strange place. On the long train journey home she eats a beef burger. *Yuk, food. Big yuk.*

She rustles under her coat in the cold carriage. Her body feels bigger. It is so obvious to her now: the way it is suddenly there, in a different form. She feels her body the whole time: her hot skin in the bath, the veins in her arms, her freezing finger-ends in the cold northern winter. It bothers her now, whereas before it was just there and it didn't matter. She hates the consciousness of it, but every time she tries to hide it, it seems to tighten its grip – telling her it is hungry, or thirsty, or fat, fat, fat. Grace covers her lap with her scarf; it feels better when she can't see it, it helps to get rid of the feeling. If she doesn't look down on it, then it isn't really there.

Grace sits on a sunlounger at her new best friend's house and they eat Pot Noodles. Grace grazes on the chicken-and-mushroom-flavour variety. She loves the taste of it, and hates it when she gets to the bottom of the pot. She tried the other flavours but they didn't match up, and so now she only eats this one, repetitively. She used to eat them without thinking, but now she looks at the hot, steaming pot and starts to think about every mouthful: every individual pea and noodle, each tiny drip of soya sauce and each fragment of chicken.

She wasn't considering food in that way before, and now she is – like in a moment she has been sucked into a different channel of thinking. And suddenly, every bit of food has a significance. Every mouthful has an important place, and she can't determine (nor does she really try to determine) how it has become like this. Every food either goes on the 'Yes' or the 'No' list in her head. Pot Noodles are on the 'Yes' list, but she is thinking of moving them on to the 'No' list after thoroughly reading the ingredients and storing information about the calorie and fat content.

Grace's best friend watches her closely. Grace can see it, because all of a sudden she is quiet and awkward-looking, like she is thinking of saying something but doesn't know how. Grace watches her back – her friend is twisting her noodles round her fork and slurping and sucking them into her mouth. She seems to be eating her Pot Noodles very slowly, Grace thinks. Grace watches how she does it, how she points her fork in the air as she makes some joke, or asks some question, between each mouthful. Grace thinks to herself that she must eat more slowly. That must be the secret of Best Friend's thinness, she decides.

'Do you want to make pancakes?' Best Friend asks. Grace explains that she doesn't want any more to eat after the big, hot Pot Noodles.

Best Friend looks at Grace and says, 'I'm worried about you. You should eat some more. You're not fat. Honestly. You're not fat in any way, not in the slightest.'

Then Best Friend rolls up her trouser leg and pinches the back of her thigh and says, 'I have cellulite too, you know. You shouldn't feel like you're the only one who feels fat, because everybody does; I do. You probably don't have any cellulite or fat, or anything like that, anyway. Yeh. Does that help? Honestly, you shouldn't worry.'

Then she rolls down her trouser leg and smiles. Job done. Best Friend goes into the kitchen, puts the pot in the bin and decides to make some pancakes. She wonders if she should, when Grace is becoming stranger, and more of a stranger every day. But she decides that she wants some. She feels annoyed that Grace can't seem to just pull herself together and eat some more, just a little bit, because she hasn't been eating enough recently, not by a long way and everyone is starting to notice, and to worry. And so Best Friend heats up the butter on the gas stove and through the kitchen window watches Grace, who is lying on the sunlounger, with her legs covered by a towel, reading through the ingredients on the outside of her tub of food.

Grace writes her diary every day. Mostly it is scribbled words about nights out and the boyfriend and moods and school stuff. Today things are different on the diary page; Grace writes something down which she can't take back. On other pages, her writing is bold, exclamatory and thrown down quickly, but on this page things are different and a bit more considered. There are big margins at each side of her writing and so the words are squashed and reduced. They are neatly and quietly formed, afraid of themselves and afraid of their admission. Grace writes her diary for a second audience, never entirely for herself. She holds things back, just in case anyone finds it, reads it and she is exposed and shown to be not as good as everyone thinks. She imagines the repercussions – of being told off, of getting into trouble for drinking, for the boyfriends, for the thoughts – so, just in case, she is careful with her words. She is careful with what she says, and what she doesn't say.

revised. Everyone doing more revision than me. Feel so fat all the time. It's so horrible. Tried to exercise but it just doesn't seem to work. I am really obsessed and I can't eat or drink anything without thinking what the calorie value is. I realize it's a big problem and as this is the first time I've written about it, I think that is good. I just can't wear any of my clothes or feel comfortable or nice any more. I'm no way going on holiday unless I feel thin. Nobody understands, all my friends worry about their weight, so to them it's like no big deal. Reassurances help a little bit, although I think I know myself better than anyone does. I really want to get it off my mind so that I can revise properly.

Grace decides not to say any more. The diet that started with eating everything but Easter eggs, then everything but chocolate, then everything but sweet things, then only pasta, then only rice cakes and tuna, no longer feels like a diet. In fact, it is no longer a public thing. It is not for anyone else's consumption. Instead, an inside voice has started to take hold. A constant pressuring, pulsing voice, which reminds her, *you are just not as good as you could be!* She weighs eight stone, then she eats a bit less and then she weighs seven and a half. Monday mornings are all about new intentions, new resolutions, further ambitions to change shape and change everything around her as a result.

I really want to succeed in these exams. It means everything.

Grace decides not to write in her diary any more. After seven years of every-day, every-night writing, she decides to hold on to her words with all the power that she can muster. She folds in her secret. She sits tight on the lid. And she tries, tries, tries to be the thinnest that she possibly can. The limits are gone. A world of eating-related happiness and unhappiness has opened up and swallowed her whole.

GAME ON

Now it's time to start the game. A chequered board. There is black and there is white. There is winning and there is losing. There is up and there is down. There are simple rules. Don't try to make it more complicated, because it isn't, not at this stage. It is like Snakes and Ladders in reverse; the winner is the one who gets to the bottom, who goes down, who slides, not climbs.

Rules:
Lower the numbers on the scales
Shrink: get smaller, smaller, smaller, smaller, disappear
And, most of all, bluff your opponents.

Are you ready, Grace?
Warning – this game is addictive and once you start you might find it hard to get away.
Squelch your fat and imagine a knife slicing right through it, cutting it off. It's good to have a visual image like that from the start. Keep it in mind and remember, if you win then everything will be OK. If your fat goes then you will feel contented. Whatever you do, don't sit still. Keep looking at your fat thighs and watch that fat blubber, lift it in

your hands, pull it and play with it. Already there is too much of it, too much of you, too much space. Look at your stomach and imagine it smaller and flatter and tighter and less present.

Tactic 1: Spin the lie:

'I'm just eating too much,' you tell yourself. 'Much more than I need.'

You must rise to the challenge, nobody likes a loser.

Tactic 2: Cut it out. Make your move from words to action. Chocolate is indulgence. If you eat it you go up, if you don't, you go down. Down is good. Less is more. Thinner is better. Thinner is success. At this stage it is important to normalize what you are doing. Give away a few details so your opponents don't guess that you might have a master plan in mind. And anyway, at this stage you can't jump ahead to more severe tactics – you haven't got that far in the game yet. So start by cutting out the sweet stuff from your diet, starting from next Monday. It's only a few, small, pointless pounds to lose.

Tactic 3: Each week drop another item from your list of consumables and see how you are racing ahead. Look at the scales. The counter is moving in the right direction – down, down, down! See how each thing you stop yourself from eating makes you feel so much better. And no one is even trying to stop you. Where is the opposition? They are miles behind. They won't resist your attempts to change because they don't understand it, so you already have a flying start. Watch them all sit back and let you get on with it. Watch them as they eat their fish and chips with Tomato Ketchup on the sofa, watch their eyes and mouths with fascination. How little emotion they display when they put the cheese on toast between the teeth and swallow in careless mouthfuls!

Can you feel that moistness at the back of your mouth? Now refuse. And all you can think about is the creamy taste of their cheese. Quickly, before you succumb, chew two pieces of gum to expel the desire. Can you feel the high?

Tactic 4: Now the game slows down. OK, so you don't have much energy, but you need to stick to the task. Just take a single plane. Focus in and don't relent. Watch how the longings to move and eat and think and do just disappear. Purify everything, make yourself purer, better. Squeeze out the fat cells one by one.

Tactic 5: You need to be quiet now. Don't make a fuss and don't let the opposition know what you are doing. This could be a fatal error. An interception now could be your downfall. One inkling of your strategy and they will be in there with the fish and chips and pasta and all the nasty things you have stopped eating. You just don't eat those things, OK?

Tactic 6: Stick to your patterns. The ones that make you comfortable. The strategies that keep you sane and driven. You need to keep driven to succeed – to be the best girl. Top marks. Top girl. You will soon find yourself waking at the same time each day, eating the same foods. There are foods now that make you feel repelled. How can people be so sloppy with what they ingest?

Tactic 7: Things are really going well for you now, but to make it better you need to bring in some exercise. Start with ten minutes a day. Exercise is a good solitary activity. Your competition is all those other fat and lazy people who aren't doing anything. Imagine them all lying on their sofas while you are succeeding, slimming and winning.

Tactic 8: BANG. BANG. I'm here. Can you hear me? I am the winning spirit. The voice to take you beyond the place you currently inhabit. Can you believe that we have become such close friends already? Thanks for inviting me in. You know that I'm not going to leave. I can't possibly leave. You opened a crack and I shifted my way into place. I am there every morning, all day and all night to help you win this. We can do it together, against them all. Best keep everything on the outside clean and tidy so no one can get through to you. I won't let them. Let's make sure it all looks spick and span. Dirt penetrates just like food, and we must keep it out. Keep the control. Don't slip. Don't make one wrong move now or it will crash BANG down. BANG BANG BANG BANG. I'm here, Grace.

Tactic 9: OK, so we need to keep this quiet. People are looking strange on the outside now. Just fold up. Folding up makes us smaller, and that can only be a good thing. That sick feeling which is permanently inside, that's me keeping the crap out. The one thing they always get you to try, especially the girls, is alcohol. Just think how bad you will feel in the morning with all that slosh inside the pit of your stomach. Become the 'friendly driver' of the group. That will make everyone like you. Stick to Diet Coke with lots of ice. Just better make sure you locked the car door. Did you lock the car door? Is it locked? Do you want to go back and check and double-check? Can't get it out your mind now, can you? Best plan the route home, and again, and have a backup, and second backup. Is it time to go already? You haven't said a word. Just keep chewing gum and playing with your mouth and your packets of cigarettes. Stop the thinking.

Tactic 10: They have got their eyes on you. You thought this was going to be easy. They were miles behind, but now they are starting to really play. You could do with taking a step back now. Move your pieces. Get out of their sight-line. Already you have to make concessions, taking the slices of toast that they offer you with a big smile. That smile really hurts. The numbers are starting to go up. They must be. It might not show on the scales but they are bound to climb if you don't keep an eye on things. Already they are trying to break the routine that you have so carefully planned and implemented. Pah. There is no way now. Not a chance. They are all too frightened of saying the wrong thing. Their hand is weak, they aren't going to show. You can carry on with your next move. They don't believe you. They don't make the connections. Congratulations. Phase one over. It is all black or white.

Black

Now it's starting to show. You feel good, don't you? There is the odd compliment, a special glance to the safety pins holding up your baggy trousers, the gaping waist of your jeans that hang from your hips. Just keep focused on the numbers. Don't worry about what people think. Keep the numbers down. Don't let them go up. Do anything before they are allowed to go up. Up leads to up and up, and suddenly you are spiralling out of control and the thought isn't possible. It is not in this game plan. THIS IS A GAME, you know. You can stop . . . if you wanted.

Just keep an eye on the others who are on the fringes of this board. Look at the girls all around you who are small and compact. Look! You are still bigger than them all. Simply compare the outlines of their forms to the obtrusive lines of your own shape: look at their small thighs, their tiny waists. Now see your curves and bumps and lines and reassert that willpower. Dig deep, Grace. Raise your game. Monday morning is a different day, a different week – a new start. Reduce your calorie intake and everything will feel different. Believe me, trust me. It will all be OK. Don't let yourself fall here; don't let them in.

I bet you feel strange. You have nothing to say. You sit and you listen in but you don't react. Watch the conversation bounce around the room. It's not interesting because it's not part of this great game. In fact, it's distracting. It's stopping you and it's taking up your time. And time is precious. You are supposed to be focusing on the plan and with all this mindless, lazy talk, nothing is being achieved. What is the point of that? So you nod and pull smiles to agree with what is being said but really you are somewhere else. You are practically floating. How does it feel to become so transparent, so airy, so bodiless? Just don't let the secret out. The feeling isn't half so good if the opposition want to join in. Leave them to their cups of milky tea and sugary coffee.

'Water, please.'

Or, even better, Diet Coke, because the bubbles make you high and light and give you a full feeling in a nice sort of way. Could something better ever be invented?

Numb the emotion. There is 'nothing wrong'. Become the bluffer; you know you can do it. They are bound to offer you food and it is easier to take it and work out a disposal method. Wrap up your pasta in a paper towel and throw it down the toilet. Take out your microwave meal, put it on a plate, eat a little and then remove a big section to dispose of into the nearest bin. Make sure it is well buried. Return with just a little on your plate to cover your tracks. Even make a comment:

'That was delicious.' See how much I have eaten!'

Even better, avoid the house at mealtimes and try and eat

only on your own. The more you get out and about, the more you can forget to eat, plus all that extra walking kills off those nasty calories.

If you are forced (with no option) to eat solid food then remember that running on the spot in the privacy of your own room can help get rid of the food: push that stuff out of your system. Push it. Squeeze it, Grace. Restrict and restrain.

If you are having a bad day, one where things are getting on top of you, then push it hard for just a few hours. You will really feel the shakes. I guarantee you will have a good day after this. Awake to forty-five minutes of aerobics and eat an apple. Walk a couple of miles to the swimming pool and swim fifty lengths then walk home and repeat the aerobics session. Can you feel the body quiver? Can you feel the shake on the inside?

Sometimes it is easier to stay inside. It is sick-making watching the outside world and all its fallacies. What is the point of caking yourself in make-up and parading through a pub? Sit tight, curl yourself up into an icy, bony ball and focus on making it right to the bottom of those scales. The world is loud and obtrusive. Watch them all letting go, drinking pint after pint, wetting their greedy lips. Lie down and feel how hard your body has worked – how good you can feel now you have battered it into submission. Lie and count the minutes slowly, one by one, and take yourself out of this world.

Of course, the quietness won't go down well. They will try and make you crack. They will suggest you aren't your-self; perhaps you are depressed? But you are *more* yourself this way, this is the real you, not the false, outward-smiling one – you know, and you control, everything that passes your lips. You know exactly what you contain, how much it weighs and how many calories there are in each thing you take in. You are so in control it scares them. They marvel at your ferocious willpower. Believe me, they will never have such willpower.

Just turn the conversation to them, put the onus back on their own messed-up, uncontrolled existences. 'Don't worry, I'm fine, honestly. I'm glad you care, but I can sort it out. Anyway, how are you feeling?' It does the trick. Put them in the position of vulnerability and watch them squirm.

Now, if you are starting to feel that things aren't exactly as you wanted, just remember the strategy. Your case is very simple. There are just a few more pounds to lose. You feel, and look, much healthier. They really can't have been looking closely before, because you had seriously chubby legs. Remind them that you know your body best and you definitely need to know it inside out. You need to make sure that if one ounce of fat develops it is squeezed out, refined, purified and beaten.

I'm here.

BANG.

White

Hazy white. Lying on the floor. Sit up and sit down and sit up and sit down. Fuzzy. Lying on the bed before sleep on the white sheet. Press up and press down and press up and press down. Things are light now. Slower, softer, gentle. La la la. Here we are. On to the next thing. Move along now. Look into the tunnel. Focus in. Walk in the white snow. Press each foot into the crisp, untouched whiteness. Lift your foot and place it down. Look ahead. Don't turn round. Just keep looking at the seamless white stretched ahead of you.

PLAY

[There are five girls sitting around a wooden table in a pub. They are eating dinner. Four of the girls are eating plates full of hot food, one girl is eating a bowl of soup. This girl is Grace. A bread roll is perched on the side of the big plate on which the soup is resting. Grace picks up the bread roll and slides it off the edge of the plate on to the table. The other girls look at each other. The table is noisy with chatter until this movement of the bread. Then Grace interrupts the silence.]

GRACE (OUTSIDE VOICE): So, has anyone got their cases packed yet? I'm going to buy mine tomorrow. Mum is taking me shopping.

GRACE (INSIDE VOICE): *Don't make me eat it. The bread roll.*

[There is silence again and then the awkward sound of cutlery indicating that each girl is eating louder and louder as if to draw attention away from the silence and towards the food.]

GIRL 1 *[bravely]*: Grace, I don't know how to say this, but do you think that you might see a doctor about things? I could come with you to see a counsellor?

GRACE (INSIDE VOICE): *Soup only. Liquid soup. No bread roll.*

GRACE (OUTSIDE VOICE): Yes, maybe. That is very kind of you.

GRACE (INSIDE VOICE): *Not even one mouthful.*

GIRL 2: Don't you want that bread roll?

[Grace looks up and down as if to try and get away from their intrusive eyes.]

GRACE (OUTSIDE VOICE) *[meekly]*: No, no thank you.

GRACE (INSIDE VOICE): *Just the soup.*

GIRL 3: Can we talk about it? I mean . . . will you be OK when you go to university? Perhaps you could see someone there?

GRACE (INSIDE VOICE): *I ate that apple earlier so I can't eat a bread roll now.*

GRACE (OUTSIDE VOICE): Sorry?

GRACE (INSIDE VOICE): *Now, how many calories could potentially be in a bread roll of this size?*

GIRL 3: About university? Will you be all right because, well . . . we are . . . you know . . .

GRACE (INSIDE VOICE): *Maybe 120? Too many, don't eat it.*

GRACE (OUTSIDE VOICE): I'm fine. I'm fine, no thank you, thanks anyway, though.

[The girls continue to eat and we see them talk to each other and to Grace but we do not hear what they are saying. Instead, Grace's voice takes over.]

GRACE (INSIDE VOICE): *I would cry if I had to eat the bread, not out loud, but inside-crying caught up in my mouth. Trapped and stuck tears in the goo of the thick, brown crusty bread. I don't want to eat it. That's how I feel. I can't. I know that something might be wrong because I feel this way, but I do eat things — certain things. They probably think that I don't. How would that be possible, not to eat anything at all? I couldn't do it. I do eat. I did some work experience this week and I ate two packets of chewing gum and Tic Tacs (only two calories each!), and an apple and a banana for my lunch. I walked round the shopping centre to distract myself from eating. Things were shivery inside and I felt a bit hollow but I didn't feel scared, not like the fear that I felt on Thursday night when people from the office took me to the pub. I ordered a jacket potato with tuna and probably butter and mayonnaise. I ate it all too, because with strange people it is harder to get away with it. Strangers make inappropriate comments and I want to make sure that they like me, so I go along with what they are doing. Also, I was starving and my tummy was hurting so I think I had to eat it. Other people in the pub had chips and greasy fried food. Then we were drinking, and at least I lost myself a bit there and felt a little bit less icy. The boy that I fancied said he fancied me back. He walked me to the bus stop and kissed me. It felt so strange, like I was floating off the ground, but not in a romantic way, more in a suspended, hovering, bodiless one. It's like the back of my eyes have melted into my head and I feel a bit more distant. That is the way it is now. No bread roll, just soupy liquid and a glass of water. I'm afraid I just can't eat much else.*

[The light is taken away from the pub table and towards a woman talking to a girl. The woman is Grace's mum. The girl is Grace's best friend. Grace joins them.]

MUM: So, did you have a good day?

GRACE (OUTSIDE VOICE): Yep. Great. Fine. We just stayed in, watched videos and went into town.

MUM [*turning to Best Friend*]: And have you eaten dinner? Did Grace eat some dinner at your house?

GRACE (INSIDE VOICE): *Don't ask her that. I'm not a little girl.*

BEST FRIEND: Yes, we did . . . she did actually. Don't worry. We had tea at my house. I'm keeping an eye on her!

GRACE (INSIDE VOICE): *Don't talk about me. It's so demeaning, having your little secret chats in the kitchen, conspiring behind my back.*

BEST FRIEND: Well, I have to go, but I'll see you tomorrow. Are you OK?

GRACE (OUTSIDE VOICE): I'm fine. I wish you wouldn't talk

about things like that. I'm OK, you know. Bye-bye. See you tomorrow.

GRACE (INSIDE VOICE): *Better alone. Be quiet. Don't give anything away. I am not a little girl any more!*

[Curtain closes.]

Four

It is a hot, slow September Saturday. Grace's head is fuzzy and empty through hunger. She has only eaten an apple today. Mum is eating lunch with her friend in the cathedral café. Grace joins them. She stares at the food and orders a large Diet Coke. She eats some green salad too. Normal enough. There is numbness in the room. Everything is at a distance removed from her body. There are conversations flying off the walls and there is noisy cutlery and an intense smell of coffee. She feels her body pulse and her head throb. She walks to the car with Mum and they start driving. They are going to buy some things for university – a suitcase, some pots and pans and plates. Grace has picked out self-catering accommodation so that she doesn't have to eat the university food. The thought of being fed, like school dinners, is too terrifying.

Grace tells Mum that she is feeling tired. Mum implies that maybe it is because she isn't eating enough and suggests that she makes her some food when they get home – some chicken and some potatoes. Grace chokes. There is a silence and a stiffening of her throat. The words get trapped. The throat won't open to breathe or speak for fear that it might ingest something impossible. Food is now an impossibility.

There are two words. Two small words, which open up a crevice of pain in the car.

'I can't.'

Perhaps if the second word had been different, the blackness/whiteness of the controlling and the not-eating would have stayed, and the game would have carried on.

Perhaps if she had said, 'I don't', 'I refuse', 'I won't', then it might have sounded like there was someone in there fighting, someone with confidence and energy, someone on a determined drive, at least someone recognizable. But now there was an admission. An admission so strange that the silence compressed the air to such a degree that everything went tight. In the 'can't' there was so little fight, so little voice. Just non-oxygenated air.

The car stops and there are tears and a strange, unallow-able conversation which suggests that somebody is angry with her. The conversation does not exist in real time, but in a blurred slow-motion where things just fall out of mouths and into space. The very presence of this conversation threat-ens everything. Grace decides to improve tomorrow – she must cut back on those apples.

Monday morning and things are grey. There is a doctor's waiting room and two parents. Then they are inside the doctor's office, and there are questions and speeches on her behalf. Everything is blank. Blank words and numbness. There is a heavy weight on her chest as she feels the walls of her breastbone stiffen. There is a prescription pad and a doctor confused by the entrance of three people who all look grey with worry, and one of whom looks very thin.

Suddenly a voice: 'She can't eat. She won't eat. At first she cut out sweets and chocolates, then all she would eat was pasta, then only rice cakes and tuna, and now . . . we should have noticed before, but we just didn't know what to look for. It seemed normal – just a diet, and then a bit more of a diet – and now we are blaming ourselves that we have watched it get to this stage. Now she just seems sad. Not herself. She is secretive and quiet; she seems to be alone more. We don't understand what is going on.'

The prescription pad is put down. Parents are ushered out. There must be a conversation because it ends.

'I think you have anorexia nervosa.'

Then there are parents again and decisions and agree-
ments.

Then there are just tears. Endless, streaming tears. There
is not even any energy to push them out; they just fall out
of her eyes apathetically.

And, secretly, there is a sense of pride and accomplish-
ment. She now has a title: she is real and authentic. If she
was an anorexic, then she was going to be the best anorexic
there could be.

They drive back home in cold silence. The noise of the
car heater drowns out the sound of their breathing. For the
first time in ages she actually isn't hungry. Her tears fill her
mouth as she sits, rocking herself in front of the fire, dribbling over a bowl of Special K.

Five

The evidence of Grace is still there: her make-up, her shoes, her toothbrush, everything still in place. The photos of her friends are stuck firmly on to the white MFI wardrobe with Blu-Tack, all smiling, all pretty, all ready. The wardrobe is filled with her clothes, hanging, not swinging, not moving at all.

There are callers for her still. There are letters marked with her name and posted through the letter box by the regular-as-clockwork postman whistling down an early-morning icy drive. Does he know? This is a place where gossip trips along the cobbled streets. He knew about her A-level results – the postman – he heard her on the radio; she was being interviewed about falling standards (an appropriate topic for someone with such high ones) and he recognized the name. She didn't like that – the lack of anonymity. Not a place for secrets or secret-hiders.

The house is now filled only by a cruel silence and an uncomfortable hovering sense of emptiness, the Grace they thought they knew now distinctly absent. Mum and Dad sit silently in front of the six o'clock news. They sip their white wine and eat their tea. There is not much talking done. There is just loss and a hole, and vacuous feelings, which come from staring into the distance for hours with tired eyes, plus a roller-coaster-style sense of a wave, or a drop, in the seat of their stomachs.

They were not really watching at first, not deep-watching. Of course, as interested and engaged parents, they were always observing, looking out for stages and changes, indications and signs, of what their children might be telling them, or not telling them. But this specific something they did not know how to look for. And when it did arrive, it took a while to be able to interpret it, and decipher what it was all about, and where it was heading. It came suddenly, over the course of a short few months. It came without warning and it came silently. So silently. She was there; a vibrant, full, loving daughter, maintaining a balanced control. She was not excessive or extreme, she was not overly rebellious, nor acutely shy and quiet, she was strong and she was fun, or so they thought. Then she disappeared behind an invisible layer – a see-through layer – and all of a sudden she was gone.

Dad and Grace go to the botanical gardens. They walk round and round. Grace feels a sort of excitement, tinged with a strange sense that she is outside of her body and that this can't be happening to her. The cases are packed, her bedroom is cleared out, she surely couldn't *not* go to university. How would that happen? How would that sort of thing work out? She has a room paid for, a place taken. What will they do when they call out the register and there is no answer to her name? What will the other students think about her? Will someone tell them the story, or will they just bypass it/her? Dad tells her that it is OK, those things will just be handled for her, because when you have anorexia people do things for you. Other people take care of the hard things, like ringing up a university and speaking to people over the phone, making cancellations, getting refunds, checking you out, without you having to do anything but listen through the door to phone conversations, where parents notify strangers of your illness on your eighteen-year-old behalf.

★

Grace lies on the beige carpet and finishes her sit-ups. She wonders what her friends are doing, the people who left her behind and went to university. It would have been her first week at university too, had this thing not got in the way. It would be Freshers' week: a new, crazy, drunken start; a new room; new people. But instead, she has a sinking sense of reversion; like walking backwards, like a video on slow rewind. Things are all out of time. And so she slinks quietly into the background of her growing-up house.

'I'm still here,' she feels like saying. 'Just a little less. A little less of me.'

But they look blankly straight through her: the pain is too much.

She wakes up to the sound of the six-thirty milkman. Her sleep is now light and fragile, like her body. It is difficult to shut down the mind at night as a headful of words cascades towards her, thoughts thumping intensely. She re-counts the day of food and drink meticulously through tables, numbers and equations. Everything has to be weighed out, measured exactly, or she feels unable to breathe, seized by an embracing panic around her throat. She feels her chest tighten with each reminder of the day's food failures, she turns over with the stabbing thought of each ingested item, aching inside with regret. Today, as always, there is no sense of quiet as she rolls over for the fiftieth time, attempting to find a position where her bones don't rub against the springs of her old mattress, and where she cannot feel every ounce of skin as it moves and slides below her.

She always wakes up this same way, startled by the light; gripped by the fear that life can possibly exist without her; her own internal and petrifying alarm rising from her stomach through her ribcage and into the base of her throat. It jolts her with its force, pushing up from within, and she is faced with an instant and horrifying reminder of her constant addiction. She simply can't lie still for long. She tries to force her eyelids shut by pressing them together with her fingers, she tries to fall back into the dream world without physicality and without contact, but she seems to physically ingest each second and choke. Stifled by her own bed she can feel only her heart as it speeds and jumps and bangs inside her, reminding her of her own flesh.

Sometimes she forgets temporarily where she is and what day it is, and she finds, in that moment – that half-second – a relief from certainty, a real breath and a sense of weightlessness. But then the voice makes its formal entrance, like clockwork. Always a dual dialogue – never any silence:

So today you are not going to have any breakfast. A banana maybe? But no, after everything you greedily consumed yesterday, it makes you feel sick. Can't you feel your legs weighing you down? Do some exercise – you can have a banana if you do some exercise.

She tries to stay in bed as long as possible, away from confronting the kitchen and the thought of breakfast, because the later she has breakfast, then the later she has lunch and then dinner, until it is so late that she won't want to eat.

She is reassured only when others eat; she likes to feed them – watching them place every crumb in their mouths, filling with fear if their plates aren't empty. She wants them to be weighed down, heavy and full, then she can be lighter and she can float above them. She can't understand the inertia that grips most people, allowing them to lounge about, uncontrolled, eating all day, every day.

Grace shakes. She gets out of bed. Taking her pyjama top off over her head she examines her body. She can see no difference; it is always the same. She puts on her cycling shorts, T-shirt and trainers, and begins her usual aerobics routine: legs, arms, stomach – a bit of everything, just to refresh her, give her a bit of energy, wake her up. Sometimes her pelvic bone rubs against the top of her thigh; that hurts a bit, but is to be expected. Sometimes the bottom of her back aches, right on the coccyx, as she lies on the floor, pushing it against the hard floor, but it has to be done; this way she will be allowed to feel worthy, worthy enough to eat. She treats herself today: only two sets of sit-ups. She is getting a blinding headache, half the room is black and blurred, a sharp piercing fuzz of the morning. She leaves the bedroom armed with her now cold hot-water bottle. Almost blinded by the pain, she can't tell anyone. There will be no sympathy – only another reason to make her eat.

Nineteen: She gets up to a tempered birthday celebration. She unwraps her presents as she shudders in front of the blazing hot fire. She looks at the faces of her family. She has failed them. She convulses with tears. She can only repeat, 'I'm so sorry. I'm so sorry.'

As they pass her the presents she struggles to gather the strength to open them. Why would anyone want to give gifts to her? She is damaging them, she is the guilty one, she deserves nothing. No-thing for her, inside or out.

They try to comfort her, throwing her a gesture, a smile or a hug, but she resents their intervention into her own mess. Their faces are stunned with pain and exasperation. The tears are welling up as she tries to breathe. She takes in air but has no room to hold it inside her. They sit and watch her, unable to move or speak, constrained by their own embarrassment and forcibly detached from her anguish. Suddenly, their strong and beautiful child, friend and sister no longer exists, all that remains is a fragile shell, held together only by her own determination. They begin to shout and scream at her because it seems to be the only thing that allows them to vent their helpless frustration, but she pushes them away, as she has always done, intent on succeeding in whatever she is trying to do, although she isn't sure what that is.

After they leave the house (for school, for work, for normal life) she fights her way through an exercise video, gasping for air as she moves up and down through her press-ups. She takes a hot bath − the hotter the better − it makes her feel as though she is cleansing out her insides. The steam and the tears redden her body. She stands up and looks in the mirror at the sinking holes in her cheeks and the blue veins jutting out of her bony arms, her dark hair layering and covering her starved skin. Until this day there has been no pain, no real pain anyway, only numbed sensations, but now there is red. Real red pain. Her body is raw and fragile and see-through. You can see the insides − the bones and the veins. The pain reaches her mouth. She coughs and shakes through the in-breaths. There is no space to breathe out.

Boyfriend arrives with a birthday present. They drive to a pub. Grace has a Diet Tango. She tells him her own diagnosis. She has given in to their decisions about her, because she hasn't got any energy left to make her own.

'I've only eaten an apple today,' she tells him. Without knowing why she suddenly feels the need to confess.

He edges a smile. 'You'll get better.'

'No, I can't. I'm not going anywhere, they're going to make me stay here.' She is crying. He is confused. He doesn't want to touch her; he doesn't know what to say. He drives her home.

They were the best couple. She liked to tell people about their 'two years together'. Because two years was a really long time, and most people only had boyfriends for two weeks, or maybe two months. He wasn't going to go to university. She liked that − their difference. She liked the way they looked together, or maybe just the look of him? She didn't really care so much how he acted, because he was hers and he was special. It was good to have a boyfriend like that, someone who everyone liked, someone a bit older, someone who didn't care about exams and university and achievement. It took the edge off her stable, reliable image. It made her seem acceptable. But when the food thoughts got in the way, things stopped being fun. He got right in the way. She didn't want him to touch her. He said things all wrong, all backwards. He obviously just didn't understand. She decided it should end and then she decided that it shouldn't. It depended on the day, on the mood, on the food. One moment he was too close, too near, too stupid, too irritating and everything seemed claustrophobic and out of control, and the next he was holding her up and she was terrified of doing anything without him. She didn't want him to go away, though. Not really, not like he did when he drove her home and then drove away, not looking back at her little body standing, staring at him through the big bay window.

Six

'How are you today?' Crossed legs, head craning towards her, the psychiatrist intrudes.

'Fine, I'm fine.'

'How has it been going this week?'

'Fine, great, a lot better.'

The psychiatrist shifts in his seat and raises his eyebrows. Grace pauses. She hates these frozen silences, when the masks come down and each one attempts to out-manipulate the other. She likes to think that she unnerves him, that she holds a secret control that is infallible; he can't touch her. She spills out her lies in his face, one by one, only small lies, but enough to make him feel that there is some improvement. She talks about herself as if she were a third person. Her 'I' is detached from her thoughts. Her 'I' is the 'I' that he wants to explore; her stomach, her insides, her guts.

She lists yesterday's food intake for him but the words get stuck in her chest. He congratulates her on the baked beans. She absorbs the words and throws them around in her head. BAKED BEANS. Beans that are baked. Beans in a metal tin. Banal baked beans. His condescension chokes her.

She sits, week in, week out, in the fusty-smelling waiting room, surrounded by old armchairs from the seventies. She reads two-year-old copies of *Woman's Own* and picks up some more diet tips: 'How I went from a size sixteen to a size ten in three months,' a beaming reader gloats, her tight perm and black leggings spruced up by the gloss of bright pink lipstick.

'I'm much better,' Grace snarls.

'Why?' he enquires

'I just am.'

Gum-chewing.

The conversation always goes this way. She, arms crossed, head bowed, lips pursed in defiance, resilient to any suggestion, blocking his interference, his constant poking into her prison.

'This is getting serious. How do you feel about coming to stay here? You do know that we can section you under the Mental Health Act, and then you will have to? It would be easier if you did it yourself. What do you think?' the psychiatrist coaxes.

She wonders how she suddenly ended up in this place with this person who doesn't know her, now wanting to get right inside her head, wanting to lock her away in the old hospital on the hill. She used to pass it on the bus on her way into town. She would conjure up images of the mad people who lived there – rocking in corners of the room, shouting out random words, on the edge. And now she is there – only a temporary visitor, but a potential future resident. It just doesn't make sense.

Her weight is dropping, not much, maybe a pound a week, but enough. Enough for him to threaten her with being drip-fed, enough to make him and his people force her to eat from their prescribed menus, like other anorexic patients. She isn't like that, no way. She doesn't want his diet plans and gold stars and public exposure. Hers is a personal and private 'illness', one the other bony girls really can't be a part of. It just won't be allowed.

'Time up.'

She is forced to make an appointment for next week. She walks up to the hatch – to the bland glance of the receptionist. It reminds her of a school canteen. She politely asks for more, please.

She walks home up the steep hill away from the hospital. The rain filters through her hood as she paces the street, moving without hesitation towards her destination. Her hair is drenched and pinned to her forehead through the heat and the moisture. The cars run alongside her, splashing up at her soles and reminding her of her presence. It is the power she gains from the control of her own footsteps and the movement of her limbs which satisfies her at times such as these. She holds her breath as fuming lorries sweep by, bellowing horns and screeching brakes sounding out. She is determined not to be slow, because she never is; the thought of minutes ticking by without her is terrifying. She feels and senses every second.

There is a feeling of momentum in every part of her body. Her fingers pulse and ache with cold, as she furrows them under the sleeves of her thin coat. Mascara is caked under her eyes, giving the impression that early that morning she stumbled out of bed without care.

The outside world now seems only a passing blur. Face-down, the pavements look the same and an unenviable greyness permeates each sightline. She is planning in detail every second of the next hour. All worked out – nothing will sway it.

She arrives home, throws off her coat, removes her shoes and goes to the fridge to get her Diet Coke. The bubbles fill her up. She likes the way it is called a diuretic, the very sound of the word makes her feel as though the inches are already falling off.

She sits on the sofa in front of Richard and Judy, the lunchtime news, the regional news, *Home and Away*, *Neighbours*; the minutes are counted one by one. No soup before 1 p.m., nothing before 1 p.m. At 1 p.m. she is allowed a treat. She prepares her WeightWatchers' soup (two varieties to choose from) and diet yoghurt (four flavours – what choice) – 150 calories altogether; she can manage 160 if she is feeling brave. At four o'clock she is allowed an apple, only a small one, weighed on the kitchen scales. She feels heavy. She wishes she had the will to be sick: throw it all up, but she can't. She tried it once; there was a splutter in the toilet, nails jammed down her throat. She could taste the soap as her fingers pushed down upon her tongue and, just at the moment of the cough, she pulled them out, her eyes red and streaming, her knuckles tooth-marked and pink, saliva dribbling from the side of her mouth. She failed. Failure wasn't acceptable.

Her mum asks her, 'You're not making yourself sick, are you?'

Teeth jam together. *I wish. I wish. I wish . . .*

'No, Mum, of course not.'

Mum looks at her disbelievingly.

Stupid girl, don't eat that tomato.

She eats it anyway. She used to be stronger than this. People remarked at her willpower before this happened. They marvelled at her resistance and jealously admired her strength. Now they retract that envy with a breath of relief at their own normality.

'So how are you today, Grace, really?' Friends tend to qualify their questions with a 'really' or an 'honestly'. She gives them what she thinks they 'really' want to hear.

'*Really*, I'm much better.'

She takes a sip of her Diet Coke and sucks on her Marlboro Light.

It is the first Christmas since the announcement of Grace's anorexic status. Six o'clock with stockings in Mum and Dad's bedroom; stockings full of presents: make-up items, chocolates, sweets and oranges. Grace still gets the chocolates in her stocking, packed in with the hope that Christmas might change her, or that for one day only she will let go, drop the fierce willpower, change the rules, stop the game or at least pause it. But she doesn't. Instead, she sits with her hot-water bottle and layers of thick jumpers, with her hands alternating their hold on the bedroom bay-window radiator. She carefully places all the chocolates, dried fruit and clementines to one side. She decides that she will give them out to others later on – 'Happy Christmas', she will say – (just because she doesn't eat, it doesn't mean that others can't!).

Grace's Christmas lunch is a salad with chopped-up tomatoes and a bit of cottage cheese and a couple of rice cakes. She also eats a bit of mashed potato (because she can feel the fire of the opposition in the deadly silence around the table). She knows that there will be much guilt later for this out-of-character mashed potato eating. Then she watches television and counts the hours until the end of the day. She can't get her exercises done because the house is full of people. She goes for a walk with Mum and Dad. She asks them if she can buy herself an exercise bike because she is sure that if she is more formally allowed to exercise, then she might find eating a bit easier. And they sigh.

PLAY ON

[A group of school friends sit around a collection of pub tables, talking and laughing, sharing stories of university and new experiences. Grace walks in. She is dressed in a bright outfit. Too bright, too present. She should be dressed in black, a symbol that she is defeated and unwell. But the bright outfit and a new haircut make a statement. The faces around her smile at her entrance. There is no outward sign of their shock. It is only when they begin to speak that there is an obvious sign of hesitancy in their voices.]

FRIEND 1: How are you?

FRIEND 2: Really like the hair.

FRIEND 3: Isn't it cold outside!

[Grace sits quietly, nibbling the straw of her diet drink. She nuzzles under the collar of her thick coat as she jitters. She is visibly shivering, although she is wearing several layers: thermal vest, tucked deep into two pairs of tights, two pairs of socks, thick velvet trousers, three jumpers and a coat. She is freezing. We see her hug the radiator, feeling her hand around it for the warmest part. The coldness produces a feeling of hollowness. She is shaking inside but she doesn't say anything. The suffering is as secret as the inside voice, which plays out over the tableau.]

GRACE (INSIDE VOICE): *So when you get home you'll go straight to bed, OK? No cereal, not one mouthful. Go in the door and up the stairs and get into bed. But I'm quite hungry, I think. Maybe an apple then? But that would mean fifty extra calories, maybe even seventy-five if it's a big one and that means one less apple tomorrow. I want cereal, perhaps? No. One bowl leads to another. No, that's it — nothing.*

[Grace is seen to join in the conversation from time to time, but everything is far-removed from her own thoughts. There are stories of drunken nights out, kebabs and sick in the street. Friend 1 pulls her aside.]

FRIEND 1: You don't look good. God . . . I hate saying that, but you were so beautiful . . . before . . . *[Friend 1 stutters over appropriate wording.]* Can't you see the difference? I mean, you're different now. Can you remember how you were before you were . . . ? *[Friend tails off.]*

[Grace nuzzles further into her coat. She looks as if she might try to finish the sentence for the friend, but even she struggles to utter the four syllables AN-OR-EX-IC which label and mark her. Her teeth are gritted, and through a plastered smile she tries to show that she appreciates the interference.]

FRIEND 1: It's just as if you've broken your leg. Like your mum told you. There is nothing to be ashamed of.

[There are glances and nervous looks from the pub crowd. Grace looks up at the TV screen. The Spice Girls are on MTV talking about Girl Power. Grace looks at their thin figures. Some people are drunkenly singing along to the music. Grace imagines their real and loud inside voices. We hear them played over the tableau on stage.]

GIRL 1 (INSIDE VOICE): *She could change if she really wanted to, the cure is surely right there before her on a plate.*
GIRL 2 (INSIDE VOICE): *Let's be honest here, this is a disease of vanity – all you have to do is eat; it isn't hard.*
BOY 1 (INSIDE VOICE): *Three times a day, taking the food from the plate into the mouth. A forkful in the mouth – a simple process.*
GIRL 1 (INSIDE VOICE): *Sympathy can only extend so far. It's hard to keep being so understanding.*

[And then we see the inside voices getting out into the room. They leak out because they have been building up. Grace's inside voice never comes out. She swallows. There is a conversation about diets and losing weight.]

GIRL 2: I haven't eaten anything all day — I just forgot!

[Grace gasps.]

GRACE (INSIDE VOICE): *How can they forget? Don't they feel the thrust of anguish, the deep stretching pain in their stomachs too? What do they do with their hunger?*

[Then crisps appear on the table and the crowd fearlessly demolish three bags. Grace watches them intensely, counting the grams of fat that they put inside them. One by one, counting, adding and totalling.]

[Curtain closes.]

Explanations

I need to stop my story here. My secret has started to unravel: one moment a child, then a teenager and then an anorexic. The expanse of time beneath these indentations of memory is so huge, and even those individual imprints upon it are murky and sporadic. There is not the control of the story that you may have anticipated. But perhaps you will also see how easy it is to be cast from one definition to another in a matter of words. One minute everything is fine, and the next, you are wondering how you managed to tear everything apart. Actions force things forward, and the grip you have on things is lost, and all at once. What you think you own, and order, and manipulate, is suddenly out of your hands.

I could leave my story this way, hurtling along from one action to the next as it was experienced, as it was breathed, memory layered upon memory, but I cannot. Because my story is a true one, it is not only inwardly folding. There are things in this story which happen in the real world, in real time, every day. There are parts of what I am telling you which need to be broken down, and there are questions which I want to answer. How did I get here? Let me take a step back.

Any parent or friend of a newly labelled anorexic must think about the possible factors that are to blame for this illness. First thoughts might be, 'Why did we not see this earlier? Why did we not know this? What could we have done to prevent this?'

I know that my parents went over and over in their heads

every possible moment or chance they thought they could have conceivably raised it with me, or tried to open me up. At the time, I would not let them get near me. I would, instead, deflect them, 'No, no thank you. Everything is fine.'

Because of my detachment from what I was doing to my body in starving myself, I couldn't have explained the reasons behind it at the time. I didn't have the capacity, I wasn't able to answer my parents' questions; I wasn't engaged with a wide enough perspective to give a proper theory on myself, a perspective which I now have.

There are so many fingers pointed when it comes to eating disorders. It seems too painful not to allot a proper explanation. Surely there is no possibility of understanding anorexia, if there is nothing to target all the pain and exasperation towards? And so it is easier to take a view. Many do. They say that it is about low self-esteem; others root for the cultural target, some to a chemical imbalance in the brain, a personality disorder, born under the wrong star sign, born too late, born in difficulty, a result of the image of thin beauty in magazines, the female brain, the media, the government, a genetic predisposition or even something more fundamental, something elemental about a renunciation of feeding. The list goes on and on and the issue becomes more and more confusing.

The most disturbing of these conclusions is seemingly one of the most prevalent among the medical profession and public – the belief that the anorexic is to blame, purposely seeking out attention through self-starving.[2]

'Silly girl.'

'Ridiculous diet.'

'One of those little phases.'

Anorexia nervosa is not about stupidity or playing up; it is an expression of something else. The body becomes a symbol to try and put across that expression, whatever it may be. The body finds a language to discuss things which cannot be articulated, or which haven't yet been acknowledged or explored.

My experience of this illness is only that — my own — but my understanding of what I went through is not confined to the edges of me. It relates to the stories of others; its sounds often resonate with theirs even if their beginnings or endings are not like mine.

So before I come to tell you more of my secret story, perhaps it will make more sense, feel less out of time, if I try and provide some reasons, some explanations, some retrospect; something to alleviate the confusion and break down the myths that surround this illness.

Growing

The doctor was able to label me anorexic because I fitted into a certain set of criteria. I was an anorexic because I:

- refused 'to maintain weight at a minimal normal level for height and age, such that the body weight is 15 per cent below that expected for the individual's height and age'
- had 'an intense fear of gaining weight and becoming fat'
- had 'a distorted notion of body shape and image', such that I 'continued to complain of feeling fat even at a very low weight'
- had 'amenorrhoea'[3]

I was no longer just a teenage girl playing with her food; I was now in a completely different territory. The above criteria tell one story of how extreme the illness is compared to someone trying to lose a few pounds, but another starting point in understanding the aetiology of the illness is that an anorexic (often unconsciously) uses food control and self-starvation to mask deep-rooted fears and feelings. These issues take refuge in the control and order of a diet and when they appear to dissipate as a result, an anorexic feels that it is definitely the self-starving that has solved them.

One of the common anxieties which anorexia works particularly hard at attacking is growth (in all senses). An anorexic circumnavigates growth or change by evading it, by stepping out and stepping back from the fear of it. This can happen at any life-stage and in either sex (10 per cent of eating disorder cases are male[4]), although the average age for the onset of anorexia is between sixteen and eighteen years. This is a time of huge physical and emotional change.[5] This transitional period involves: leaving home, moving away from what childhood represents, and developing sexual and adult relationships – changes which many teenagers feel they don't know how to handle.

In post-pubescent anorexics, weight loss is often a physical manifestation of the rejection and fear of growing up. During puberty, the body changes. In girls, body fat increases to provide the tissue for fertility and menstruation.[6] Anorexia forcibly stops this growth and reverses it; amenorrhoea (absence of menstruation) occurs and the body slides back to a pre-pubescent state. Physically, the anorexic is stating that she doesn't want to be, or look like, an adult.

In my case, at eighteen years old all of a sudden, I didn't feel right about impending adult changes in my life. I felt uncertain about things, I felt there would be no going back to my own bed, in my own home, where I had lived all my life with my brother and sisters and my mum and dad. I felt like things were shifting and moving and growing, and I wasn't sure I was ready to grow with them. Whereas some people, when they are dealing with adolescence and growth, go out and rebel, or become moody, smoke, drink or take drugs, I did not know what to do, I did not know how to react. I did not feel that I should react, being the gold-starred girl that I was. There was a vulnerability within me, which was exposed and which meant that I was less able to deal with taking ownership of the changes within me than other people going through the same experience. Paradoxically (and anorexia is full of such paradoxes), I was desperate for my independence, but the freedom I so craved was a theo-retical one. I believed myself to be mature but it was an intellectualized independence, not a practical, lived-through one. (I passed my driving test but was scared of driving, I achieved my A levels but wasn't ready to go to university.)

A flicker of my fear turned to action and into a controlled, rigorous diet. The initial diet, I thought, was a means to lose a bit of weight but, in fact, it became more about evading the pressure and anxiety in my life. Focusing on my gradual path to self-starvation made me feel better temporarily and therefore, I thought, better able to deal with my life changes, but in fact it was the inverse.

The question is then why did I, and many others, use self-starving as the supposed answer to that uncertainty? A part of this answer tends to come straight to the issue that in our society being thin means being popular (very important things to a young person). The answer to all the growing-up issues is simply and neatly packaged in a smaller, more slender body. It is an answer that is also dangerously internalized. A diet might be discussed, but anorexia is rarely something shared with friends. It is a secret, personal and private territory. In fact, many teenagers seem to identify with the sense of cerebral and bodily enclosure that anorexia effects. Some anorexics have written about how special they think they are and how anorexia has answered their feelings of being detached and disengaged from the world. I think this has led to a horrible glamorization of eating disorders and of being young, thin and aloof. I have heard and read on more than one occasion about young teenagers who have admitted to being inspired to actually start an eating disorder. They have recognized a set of feelings about the world in other anorexics' descriptions, and have made some sort of confused decision from there, without understanding what the dreadful implications are. Anorexics come to the (wrong and misplaced) conclusion that their shape is their identity, and that it is their shape that controls their future. Of course, it does end up controlling their future, but in the most destructive and irreparable way.

For me, it was not such an informed decision as deciding to imitate someone else. I feel that the best explanation is that one day my view of the world changed. I suddenly had a concept of the presence of myself, and with this a raft of emotions, and I didn't know how to handle it. What I knew, what I believed in and what I trusted was the home that I grew up in, the family I was nurtured in and the small town that cushioned me. Then, all of a sudden, I felt transplanted. It was all too much: the decisions (no longer imaginary, but real, adult ones) and the size of everything facing me. And so I disengaged from feeling. It was not conscious. It was not as if I made a choice to starve myself based on a considered self-awareness. I was just struggling to find my place, like anyone experiencing change and growth, and nothing seemed certain any more, except what I did or didn't eat.

Addiction

My anorexia did, on one level, start with a diet, but it quickly turned into an addiction. One minute I was counting Easter eggs and the next I was on a path to self-destruction. Something happened, something clicked when my relationship with food changed from one of routine and normality to one of denial and control, and it spiralled from there. Food, and my focus on avoiding it, was suddenly an all-consuming obsession. My immense, and often overwhelming, hunger for success, perfection and achievement was forcibly quashed by this new focus on the suppression of my appetite. The more I fought my hunger for food, the more my desire for everything else disappeared. Suddenly I was totally trapped and addicted to this new relationship with food and could not begin to understand how that was the case.

From a physical perspective it is possible to explain how, under the effect of self-starvation, the brain becomes obsessed with food. When the body is satiated it can relax, it can sleep, whereas when the body is hungry, its response is to be awake, on the alert for potential food sources. This leads to fantasizing about food, thinking about it constantly, even dreaming about it because the body is craving.[7] I would dream of roast dinners, my mouth crammed with food, bursting with it. I would wake up, petrified that this might have been a reality, and take a huge breath of relief when I realized it was only a dream. It could be argued to some extent that this can happen even on a diet, so how did a diet, which supposedly has the focus of looking and feeling better, collapse into anorexia which has such self-destructive objectives?

Being anorexic means being constantly fixated with food; it takes over and, crucially, it doesn't stop. This is very different from a diet, which has an ending, which is set in a finite term: 'Drop a dress size in two weeks.' 'Get a bikini body in seven days.'

A diet comes to a close, until the next one begins, whereas anorexia is never satisfied by such a completed goal. It presents the sufferer with the feeling that 'if only' more weight were lost, then everything would be OK. The problem is that this resolution is rarely reached. This is why the definition of anorexia nervosa – that absence of appetite – is so misleading, because it is in fact a continual, endless and ever-present obsession and interest in food, body and weight. The appetite is there, most definitely – it is just too dangerous to let loose and so every energy is focused on stopping it.

Most importantly, what happens at the start of an addiction to not-eating, and in my case to a restrictive eating disorder, is that it seems to act like a panacea. I felt better when I ate less. My addiction to not-eating was actually an addiction to feeling better, to feeling fixed. I also had very low self-esteem, in common with many people who develop anorexia. Beneath the layers of the achieving, accelerating Grace, there was an inner lack of self-confidence. It so happened that food restriction was the mechanism for me that initially helped me feel less fragile, and triggered this change of mood inside.

The initial buzz that not-eating provides is something that I often hear repeated. Take two girls talking about fasting, about restriction, as a means of finding themselves and feeling better:

'It's amazing. It's like I'm a different me. I'm superwoman when I'm fasting! It helps, with everything.' The faster casts a wry smile.

'But don't you get hungry and need energy to live a normal life?' The listening girl is intrigued.

'I feel a bit spaced out when I do it. I can't concentrate on problem-solving, that type of thing, but I totally escape myself. It's a freeing feeling.'

I can recall the beginning of my addiction to not-eating. The feeling of lightness – of happiness – and a fuzzy, airy kind of an energy, which seemed to be irreplaceable. This is the high – every addiction has one – something that makes you feel good, something that is worth the low, or so it seems. Initially, my addiction brought me power and pleasure. With each new shape I made for myself, I was more optimistic, more alert, more euphoric and more in charge. I ended up feeding only from my addiction. I was surging off the highs that my super-control gave to me.

Power and Control

Those suffering from eating disorders often feel that they have walked into a relationship with food they did not choose. They feel that it took them over and that they are suddenly powerless to its effects. They didn't mean to get addicted, they didn't mean to lose so much weight; they didn't mean to interrupt everyone's lives, not on purpose, anyway. At the same time, however, they also feel a sense of immense control over their relationship with food. Whereas other issues and decisions might seem overwhelming and unconquerable, food is manageable and can be manipulated by the sufferer. Anorexia moves life into a restricted pattern of behaviour based solely around food and exercise. It means a regression into a simple, straight, black or white way of living.

In my experience, my food patterns gave me comfort – there were answers to problems. There were merely shapes – shapes of me – that told me how good or bad I was feeling and this reassured me. Not-eating seemed to work like a magic trick – the more I restricted myself, the more I sensed my own power. I also developed a feeling of righteousness about what I was doing. Controlling and restricting my body empowered me with a code, a way of fixing and structuring anything that was thrown at me.

In fact, many anorexics, when forcibly taken to the doctor for a diagnosis (as often happens), can only see the positive in what they are doing. They feel that other people simply misunderstand them, because there really is 'nothing wrong'. They are acting to expectation, they are being 'healthy' and 'fit' and 'thin'. They are not shovelling fast food into their bodies and eating all the 'wrong things'. They are in control, right?

However, whereas their friends who count their WeightWatchers' points or watch their GI levels are conforming to other people's patterns, and obeying the most current world order, an anorexic is actually defying it, and making up a set of her own rules. A diet is acting to a set of prescribed rules laid down by a book, a magazine or a slimming club. It is about participation and regulation. An anorexic does not want this direction from the outside. She wants control of her own game, thank you very much.

I certainly did not want any help with my anorexia. I knew that what was happening to me wasn't right but I couldn't get past the feeling that I had everything in place just as I wanted it. Any discussion of interference into my way of handling it was terrifying and inconceivable. I was petrified that if I didn't keep my hunger under control everything would collapse.

My memory of this time is dominated by impressions of figures from the outside of my anorexia trying to do exactly that: aiming to disrupt my self-control. There was a constant intrusive presence of psychiatrists and nutritionists, family and friends, intent on taking away my internal power, which I found and owned for myself, focusing on spoiling the lines of the character of Grace I had so neatly sculpted. And because none of us had the same shape in mind for the outcome of things, I used whatever power I had to fight them, not the eating disorder. I drew an invisible circle around myself. If I didn't share anything of myself – no words, no thoughts – then I was convinced that I could continue on my own.

The amazing thing about the initial stages of anorexia is that it does seem to imbue you with a surge of physical power. In eating less and less, it appears that you have more energy. The restlessness and the anxiety, which come from the hunger, translate themselves into a jittery, edgy, get-up-and-move impulse, which only drives you further. Then, all of a sudden, the illness begins to consume you, and while the body consumes very little, it consumes you even more, and so you become encircled by it, by a fear of losing control, a fear of letting go of this hold over your weight, over food and over everything. Then it becomes all quiet and blank, and you feel like you are floating out of your body, above people's voices, detached from the world. To engage you need to be able to feel, and when feeling is too difficult, there is shutdown and closure, and days which pass by without any thought external to that of the body and how to suppress it; how to keep it under further pressing control. So instead of empowering you with total control of your every move, the reverse happens. You look like a child, you appear small and childlike and so that is how you are treated.

Within a matter of months, my invisible circle got so big that I would barely let anyone touch me or talk to me. If I did talk, it was all on a top layer, on a level which didn't get near my skin, a level which was not a part of me, but was external to me. The more that I continued to starve – in fear, in addiction, out of control – the more I became alienated from myself. I wasn't even able to remember what I used to talk about, think about or how I even started to think or talk from the inside. No, suddenly it was all from the outside. I was talking for the poorly me because she wouldn't talk, in the way that someone might try and voice the feelings of an elderly person who they falsely assume has no right or ability to speak for themselves.

'No, she doesn't want any food, thank you very much.' Perhaps the self-alienation was the only way of coping. I was removed out of my own pain. It wasn't happening to me but to a version of me and so it was almost bearable.

In my interpretation of this time, I see what the doctors and psychiatrists tried to do; how they were trying everything they knew to change me or to move me. But I have the power of the whole in my hands now. I have the power of hindsight, retrospect and reason. The memory must remain as it was, framed in anger and pain and with a critical edge, where the hospital and the waiting rooms and the cottage cheese talks are seen out of focus and in one dimension. This is the only way to truly see inside the anorexic mind and to break through the invisible circle which deflects away those who try to travel inside it.

Bearing Witness

An anorexic uses her body as a vehicle for expression of emotion, fear or anger, and in this she implicates those looking on. History provides us with many examples of people using food and appetite as a voice in different ways. The suffragettes used hunger-striking as a political instrument; in religious contexts, food abstinence has been an articulation of repentance or atonement. It is a powerful weapon, a weapon of demonstration, an act of implication, used in a variety of cultural situations.

It seems that many adolescents who develop an eating disorder like anorexia are unconsciously using it to express their feelings, often towards their families. Some theorists believe that there are personality traits that many people who develop anorexia nervosa have in common. One of these is a wish to please their parents and to be universally liked.[8] A result of this is that they have not allowed themselves, or been allowed, to express feelings of anger or upset, nor have they felt that they have the voice to do so. Many parents of anorexic children will say that those daughters and sons were obedient, quiet, loving, good children when they were younger.

That goodness, which the anorexic feels is so much a part of everyone loving her, means that she will do anything to keep up a polished exterior. This is the way she has learned that things work, and the whole family learns the same pattern. Because of this, the anorexic chooses a silent and secretive way of demonstrating her feelings; she keeps her secret starving to herself so as not to cause harm, not to displease. She makes a statement, she thinks, in the nicest and quietest way possible. In retaining that goodness, and in not talking about issues of frustration and anger, a sense of pride is retained. Pride (such an important and precious feeling to an anorexic) is still intact in not-eating, but more talking is actually done through this act than has ever been done before. She slowly tips the balance of power; she asks to be recognized and she asks to speak.

'Confront me and my power on show,' she challenges.

'Witness me,' she says.

I did this. I asked my family and my friends to watch me self-destructing – I made them, forced them. I sat them down in front of me and I carried on. We watched each other over the dinner table. I tried to pretend that I wasn't interested in my plate at all, and that I couldn't stand the idea of food, but instead it was really the opposite. I was counting the seconds until each meal, I was blisteringly aware of the size and shape of every crumb on my plate and on theirs. I suppose – without knowing – I wanted my family to witness this thing that was happening to me. I wanted to tell them that I couldn't cope, but that I was not sure why I couldn't cope or what the problem was. I needed somebody's shoulder to cry on, but I did not want to cry out loud. I was so proud of my status, my achievements and my successes that I did not want to admit any fallibility. I wanted to be strong, and in my not-eating I was stronger and more resilient than they had ever seen me, but I was also forcing a confrontation. I was forcing a conflict. I was refusing to eat their food.

The hardest thing must have been that they were not able to give me a plaster, a bandage, some Calpol or a cool flannel; instead, they had to watch me be ill, and not do anything immediate about it. Inside their heads, and in the meetings with the psychiatrists, nutritionists and family therapists, and in endless conversations with friends, with experts – with anyone who might have any idea about what was happening to me – they just wanted to know what they had done wrong and how they could help.

Harder still for my parents was that the treatment I was initially offered was limited and they were left powerlessly watching from the sidelines (anorexia is particularly good at alienating those around it). As with many eating-disorder patients, the first stop was my doctor's surgery. I was lucky that the GP I saw that day was sympathetic and that she immediately saw the signs. Perhaps this was because I was not as advanced in my illness as others, whose levels of secrecy and closure prevent GPs being able to diagnose correctly.[9] I was more open; I was falling and ready for someone to catch me. The next stop (and the only free one available to me) was to be an outpatient at the local psychiatric hospital. This immediately threw me. I didn't see anyone else like me, and I didn't know why I was sent there. It made me feel worse. Unfortunately, this is the norm for many patients, because provision in specialist centres is so sporadic, and because even where there is provision, waiting lists are long, leaving the sufferer to shrink, the problem to grow and the parents to simply, wearily and desperately hang on.[10]

It must have been impossible to watch this, to witness this. The consequences of the illness are potentially enormous: anorexia has one of the highest rates of mortality for any psychiatric disorder.[11] If unresolved, the end result of anorexia is death. This is not a shock statement, it is a reality: up to 20 per cent of those seriously affected die, and rates of suicide are cited as up to 200 per cent higher than in the general population.[12]

Like nineteenth-century hunger artists who starved themselves and then displayed themselves as living skeletons, gawped at by people who paid to see these miraculous figures on show, I made my body into a performance.

'Here I am.' I didn't say, 'starving myself'.

'Here I am.' I didn't add, 'not eating my dinner'.

'Now watch me.' I didn't exclaim, 'throwing my pasta down the toilet!'.

'And for my final trick of the evening – 200 sit-ups on a totally empty stomach. Thank you, ladies and gentlemen, mums and dads, boys and girls, and goodnight.'

'Ta da.' (Circus round of applause.)

Memory

As my body began to close down all functions that weren't critical to its survival, I think it also stopped me remembering my experiences. It was like there was not enough weight to support them. My focus was so single-minded and so food-driven that the events and the people who surrounded me barely existed in that same time. Because a lot of my actions were not conscious, breathing ones, they were not admitted. I can find them only through thinking of a face, name, room or date, or by flicking through old letters and photos.

In the telling of my memories, it is not always possible to write them as if they were lived and breathed in fine detail. The detail could be made up, of course. The memoir would then become full and lifelike; like a beautifully crafted novel. You would see subtle angles of light, floating through windows; I would present you with puffs of cigarettes dissipating into the thick air. The text would be cluttered with the landscape of description. This is not the memoir of a full brain, but the memories of a fog-filled one. My narrative is fragmented because my sense of self was fractured. It is this that I am trying to reflect. Lucidity and clarity aren't available when, as an anorexic, you are totally self-absorbed, unable to contemplate living without your addiction.

In the memories that I do manage to capture – those days, hours or minutes that I did hold on to – I have to look through a further layer; that of myself looking in on myself, far-removed from the space in which I lived. I did not feel the moment, but I acted as if I was ahead of it, almost as if I was trying to control time. The only way to deal with the pain of the starving and suffocated body was to step out of it and make every thought a rational one. I was a protagonist in a rather difficult situation, dealing out my lines with composure and authority.

Sometimes the memories I am unlocking are viewed from such a distance that the scene is shown and the faces of the characters are visible, but only certain colours are clear. I am in a pub, sitting with my friends, and all I can see is a bright striped cardigan that I am wearing, and a grey-looking smoky surrounding. I am listening in on the conversations but my hearing is impaired by the noise I was then making to block things out. Characters enter and converse, but what they are saying is muffled. I wasn't really listening to anybody else – not properly – so nothing registered. I was held fast in my own world and all entrances were blocked. It is frustrating. The colour of my cardigan diverts me off course; it is blinding.

I can only build the scenes in my memories from the fragments of senses to which I am allowed access. The cold is always there. Real chilling-to-the-bone cold. The cold that comes when the circulation is motoring so slowly that it barely moves; instead it conserves the energy it requires and it reduces and reduces more. The painful cold is the only thing I can really feel, apart from the noisy, unremitting, whirring inside voice, which speaks so quickly and constantly that it leaves no room for analysis. It is all about action. People aren't even recognizable as individuals. They are simply voices which ring with no particular accent, just one of intrusiveness. They are always interrupting because my inside voice seems to be in permanent conversation. Outside voices want to talk about their angle on things and whatever they want to say is always wrong, always out of time.

My memories are not one voice. When we listen to or

watch our memories they come back in different ways. Stop and listen to one. Furrow your brow and go deeper. Sometimes it is a voice or a sentence that repeats itself over and over. Sometimes you are part of the action, sometimes you are watching through your own eyes. Sometimes there are pictures and no words at all – flashes of things, which pass over space and then disappear.

Putting these memory-stories down on paper gives them a firm reality. Things have come to light in the writing. Emotions that weren't accessible then have begun to live. The very act of telling this secret story has sparked the regeneration of lost thoughts and feelings.

I can now hear my voice.

PART 2

This Is I

This Is I

When I wake up in the morning I think
today is going to be a better day
I can look after myself
Sorted.
But bed is relief away from taste and body
until I wake again with fresh intentions
and broken calorie counts.
My heart is pushing down on my ribcage
in between bouts of hysteria my mind
is so quiet
that it feels as if it no longer
exists?
The lyrics of their tongues seem so out of tune
and pound against my head.
Leave.
You are crushing my skull and there is no
direction left to fight.
You want answers, emotions, feelings –
hissing reverberations of your endless questions.
I clasp at a fistful of air
a cigarette
lines of reasoning
Diet Coke.
You are unconvinced.

Seven

'Why do you think this happened?'
   'What are you angry about?'
   'Is it something from your childhood?'
   'Stop closing up.'
   'Are you making yourself sick?'
   'Are you taking laxatives?'
   'What are you really upset about?'
   'You are projecting.'
   'Who are you, really?'
   Whitecoats. You do wear white coats. But I can see that underneath you are wearing real clothes. In the meantime I am wearing white all the time, because everything is fine. Surely your theories are wrong. There are no bad memories. I'm not a victim of abuse/bad parenting/neglect. I feel guilty taking up your time. This NHS treatment isn't easy to come by. Please take it to someone who needs it. I'm sure you can see that I am handling this. It can't always be to do with beginnings, like you think. Sometimes things just happen, people are just made that way, it is a matter of personality. I will work it out. Thanks, anyway. I have read all the books and the leaflets, please don't patronize me by telling me why I am here. Your psychoanalysis doesn't work with me. I am a typical case. I'm well educated, well loved, a high-achiever. That's why. I get it. It's all so obvious to me. You don't need to explain. I know you like the text-book cases. It must make you feel like you are on top of this whole thing. I'm not so sure you are. I think you are beleaguered by the fact that I am not going to let you in.

Please don't devalue me by comparing me to the others. Their stories are different. Your white coat doesn't make you an expert on me. You will never be that, because I won't allow it. I know how you like me to go back and talk about my childhood. I just shrug my shoulders. I can't help you. You're getting colder and colder. Not a very good detective, are you? And, by the way, the books you gave me to read have been most helpful. I have seen where the others have gone wrong. They give me the insider tips. I won't let those kinds of mistakes happen to me. I have a huge knowledge base. What about you? I can tell you the calorie content of any food and any drink. And I am exact about it, I don't round things up or down. It's all very precise.

You know, it's funny because I actually like white. It's pure and clean and empty, but the way you wear it! Oh, you make me laugh. But seriously, I do need you to get out of my space. I'm starting to feel really claustrophobic. I keep running but it doesn't seem to make things better. There is you and your white coat, and then there are the others, in their white Fiestas whistling at me through their car windows, blasting their music out, piercing my ears. I can't stand the intrusion of them, you see – the way they look at me (or used to) – not any more, thankfully. I am just trying to push myself a bit further and you are all distracting me. And, of course, there are my lovely, loving parents. Who, in their own unknowing ways, are trying too hard to play me at my own game. They buy me whatever I want. I could order any food from anywhere in the world, and they would make sure I had it. I hate that. I hate the fact they think they know what I will eat, and what I won't. I am an adult! They even buy me rice cakes. I don't like it that they know that I eat rice cakes. It was my secret. It's like I am giving the game away. I need to change tactics. We all have to sit at the table eating together. They, with their Sainsbury's ready-made Indian meals, and me with my pile of lettuce. What a charade. Let's not sit here, pretending this is normal. I know what they are trying to do. It's what you have told them. I can see you coming through them. They are just the bodies to carry your message home when you are not there. It is all so damn facile. I have seen your ideas in my house. Mum returns from the supermarket with every low-fat/low-calorie dish on offer. 'Count On Us' – I would rather not! I can't believe people actually trust these products. How can you be sure that they have counted every calorie correctly? I see how you are attempting to shape me again. You may try, but I am the artist of myself.

And now you have got another of your cronies on board. A lady who makes me write down everything I eat. She makes lists of things that I should eat, and I don't eat them. What is the point of that? To make me feel humiliated? Well done. You have humiliated me. I don't think anybody is laughing. The worst thing is that the lady is so nice. I don't do nice at the moment. I'm sorry. So you are all there, looking at me, observing me, trying to work me out and I'm not really interested. I can't look at any of you any more.

Everybody stares, and sometimes I don't even notice. People are always around me; they don't dare leave me on my own. They watch me sip my soup, looking on and devising ways to try and feed my little body. I am seeing only inwards. Inwards is absorbing. Outside there is nothing for me. Nobody gets it, only the insides understand. They are not even being nice to me, you know. A lot of the time there are people screaming at me. They tell me that I have messed everything up. I have caused this big dent in the family. I just want them to ignore it. Why can't they just ignore it? I will get it fixed for them. OK, all right, sorry. Yes, I take the blame. Just don't bring it up, please. Don't mention how you can't work, think, sleep, even eat, for

God's sake, with this on your mind. I am not used to this. I am a nineties child. I don't expect to be fed; I opened the door with my own key when I came home from school. Can you believe it! I made my own meals. And now I cut and chop in meticulous detail. Everything I make is quite beautiful.

The highlight of my week is going to the supermarket. It is a frantic, heart-pumping experience. I am on a high. If only I were let loose on my own, then it would be uncontrollably good. I could spend hours finding out more about my specialist subject. Put me on *Mastermind*. I would memorize the contents of the entire supermarket. At the moment I am forced to rush around and pretend I am not interested. Do you know what it feels like when the extra low-fat cottage cheese is missing? They don't think of people like me and our needs. My stomach rolls. And the trouble with the supermarket is that I have to bump into people I know. There is no room in this squeezed-up town. More starers. Last week someone hurtled up to me with her trolley, her face full of pity.

'How are you feeling?' Head tilted.

I hate the concern. It's so embarrassing. They seem to think I have failed. I reply mechanically, I project what they want to hear. I don't want to make any more people worry than is necessary. I disconnect from the thought.

'I'm fine, thank you.'

Mum strides up behind me and pounces. 'No, you're not. What are you talking about? She's not fine and she's not OK.'

Lady with trolley looks taken aback. She didn't need to hear. People don't. Not when they are in Sainsbury's. They don't know what to say. Embarrassed well-wisher has not expected this response and says her pitiful farewells. It is really humiliating. There you go – I have engaged with a feeling. You must be pleased. My eyes even heated up so much I almost cried. I never cry in public. I almost exposed myself. I almost let them prick me. And I don't fight back when they shout at me because I can hardly open my mouth any more – words slice through my throat.

I cried today. I won't tell you I did, like I won't really tell you what I think, but between me and me, today I really cried. I don't cry because I am not sure I will be able to stop. Like if I lie down, I might not be able to ever get up again. Like if I eat . . . well, you know . . . where are the limits and where are the edges once you decide to let go?

So, Dr Whitecoat, what do you make of me?

This is I.

Eight

I have seen the photos of me. They show me them, to help me see better. All I can see are the fat bits. Their mouths fall open.

'How can you?'

How can I? That's what I see. I suppose the rest of me doesn't look particularly pleasant but that is why I cover it up. They don't usually take photos of me, anyway. They probably don't want to indulge me, not in any respect. The other day I found some trousers that actually fitted me. Mostly things are hanging off my hips, which is annoying because I can't really go shopping, but these size six trousers were perfect. I couldn't believe it – I had halved my size. Size twelve made me feel far too big. Not allowed! But six! Even though I bought some nice trousers, Mum wasn't happy which is unusual because we have always loved shopping together – but not any more. They are some black, thick, velvety trousers. I will have to wear them every day because I do not have any other ones. Size six!

I stare at photos of me aged six years old. I was so pretty then, and so thin. I wonder if I was always going to have fat thighs and hips, or if I could have avoided it. I turn the photo all around to look at the different angles of my childhood body. If only I could have made myself eat less, or exercise more, then maybe I would have had thin thighs now. I should have tried harder in PE, like my teacher said. I should have tried harder at cross-country running. In fact, maybe I should do some running? If everyone stopped watching me for a second, then I would get some space to run. I would like to run long distances, so I could forget myself.

I can't really find a proper image of me, which is frustrating. Every mirror seems to tell a different story. In the changing rooms I shrink and grow from shop to shop. They are trying to fool me. I know their tricks. They make me appear taller and thinner, longer, more stretched out. I like to look at other girls in the changing rooms and examine their shapes, so that I can compare them to mine. It helps me think about how I must work harder to be more like them. I am sure that my real, true, perfect shape is out there somewhere, and one day I will get it, and fit into it, and be happy in it, and things will feel better.

It is just better to be lighter. I am sure that many people feel this. You feel so much clearer, as if nothing weighs you down. You can almost stop the thoughts of anything bad or scary (except the food, of course). You float along, and all the other silly fears evaporate around you. I know I don't entirely see straight, but it's the clearest sight I have had for a long time. It's unimpinged on by other things – there is one direction and one focus, and everything else has sort of melted away.

The doctors and the well-wishers try to make me see things through their eyes, as if mine can't be trusted. I can't let that happen because I can't see round the corner of their plans. With my way I know where I am going; I know that with every pound/stone/kilo/ounce that comes off, things feel better. The other way will feel bad. It will feel worse every day with every extra pound/stone/kilo/ounce that they make me put on. They will have to *make* me do it, because I won't concede.

I don't usually like breaking the rules like this. I don't like getting told off. I got told off once or twice at school for putting on make-up or for wearing a round-necked jumper instead of a V-necked one, and I didn't like it. I tried to smirk and smile, and be disobedient to fit in, but I didn't know how to do it, it's not in me. Now people are treating me like a naughty girl. I let everyone down. I ruined their plans for me. I made everybody cry. But I didn't mean for it to happen like this. I am not very good at fighting with the outside. The fight is inside, and it is with myself.

My English teacher from school even calls me up at home and asks me why have I done this to myself (people do, they can't help but wonder). It is really embarrassing because I was always a really good student. He sounds vexed because I have spoiled things. The school sent me a book token with a special bookplate: a prize for being the best English A-level student. I wonder if they gave it to me as a badge of sympathy. I stuck the bookplate into a new, crisp, hardback book, but I don't seem to be able to read it now. My teacher is kind, but I don't want him to be like that, full of sympathy and confusion because I am quite clear, not confused. And he asks me, 'How did this happen?'

And I tell him, 'Well, the doctor thinks it is because I am a perfectionist.'

I think that this is a good interpretation of me, and one which my teacher will be pleased with (clever girl, I think to myself), but instead he says, 'You wouldn't think you were a perfectionist, not by looking at your handwriting.'

Then he sort of laughs a bit, because he is uncomfortable (I think), but he also thinks that he has made a good joke. I don't laugh, because I think he is right; I don't dot the 'i' on perfection and perhaps I should try harder to do so. I really should work on my handwriting. Then we say goodbye, and I think that this is all mixed up. I have left school, and I should be at university now. Then my teacher speaks to my mum, and it is embarrassing, for him to be talking to her about me, because I am no longer a school-girl; that girl in the uniform is behind us both.

'Get well soon,' he says.

'I will,' I say.

Nine

The plan is as follows:

Exercise = 40 minutes a day
Reading = 2 hours a day
Television watching = 8 hours a day
Eating = 20 minutes a day
Sleeping = 10 hours a day
Thinking = 2 hours a day
Cleaning = 1 hour a day

I don't like to be disturbed. I like to be in this place, at this time, that is how I like things. Please do not try to move me. My Cindy Crawford aerobics video keeps me sane, and yet I have to practise it while everyone is out of the house because they think it is damaging me. I alternate between the two forty-minute workouts. I know the entire sequence, every word that is said and every beat of the music:

'This exercise is really great for this little muscle in here' (model points to top of thigh, I point to top of my thigh), 'and one, and two . . . and twenty.'

I think it must be one of the better videos, because you actually feel it deep in your muscles. I don't dare try any other tapes in case they don't work, and then I will have wasted my exercise time. I think that if it hurts, it means that it must have some impact. NO PAIN – NO GAIN (or weight loss, in my case). I feel such satisfaction when my muscles ache and pulse with pain, and when it feels as though I am tearing my heart out. It is the first thing I think of in

the morning and the last thing I think of at night. I think
about it all day in between, too. I don't understand why
they try and stop me doing it. I am making myself fit. I
sometimes wonder if they know that I start exercising the
very second they leave me on my own. As I watch the car
pull away, I jump into my cycling shorts and press 'play'.
Sometimes they seem to come back just to check on me.
This is so frustrating. I have to stop the tape, pull off my
trainers and hide them behind the sofa, run to the bathroom, wipe the sweat from my face and pretend I have been
lying there on my bed (like the way they want me to be),
doing nothing. They want me to do nothing, so that I don't
use up any energy. My bottom is hurting from the hours I
have spent lying and sitting down. I need this workout to
refresh me. I need this to make me feel something, otherwise I feel disgusting and heavy and flabby.

They prefer it when I read. 'Reading is motionless,' they
tell me. 'Reading can help you relax.'

I sit there, pen in hand, analysing the text. I do not relax
when I read. I think of achieving. I think of how I need
to be better, and know more and be more intelligent. I now
have doubts about going to Bristol University where I should
be right now. I was only going there because of its Olympic-
sized swimming pool and the gym's easy access – all so I
could make sure I got plenty of exercise. I know they say I
won't go to university anyway, not even next year, but I
don't think like that. I can't think like that, like I can't eat
chicken and potatoes. I have been reading about Cambridge
University. This seems like the ideal place for me. Now this
illness has happened to me, it must be this way for a reason.
If I have to be away from university for a year, missing out
on all the things that my friends are doing, then when I go,
I want to go to the best place possible. So I sent away for
the prospectus. The college at Cambridge that I like has a

gym actually on site – it's ideal! Of course, they are all speechless. Mouths drop. Eyes bulge. Tears form. They don't even congratulate me on making such a brave decision. They almost refuse to take my application form to school to get a reference from my old sixth-form head of year.

'Of course,' they say, 'we will have to ask him to mention your illness on the form.'

'Of course!' I say.

My form is perfect. I have typed and retyped and retyped and retyped it. It is neat and tidy and faultless. He can mention my illness if they want, but my perfect form to Cambridge is in the post.

I tell them not to interfere. When they start to meddle I just step up the pace. They can't understand the way I order things. I like things in order. Faultless. I like things done in a special way, or I get into a panic. It is the way I am. I have always been a person of routine. I am a creature of habit. It makes me feel better. I like to know how my day is planned. I know it all inside out. They don't like this at all. They want to be part of it and so try and give me suggestions of things I should add to make my life more normal, more like theirs. I think this is their way of dampening their own guilt. It's like my kind of control isn't acceptable. You can hear it in the voices of strangers when I tell them I don't drink tea or coffee and, 'No thank you, I don't drink alcohol either.'

They find it too difficult. They can't understand how I can possibly be so restrained.

'Don't you miss food?'

'Doesn't this cake smell lovely? It would taste so good.'

No thank you. Blocked out, blocked out.

They convince themselves that I must break off from time to time. I must give in and join them in their weaknesses and addictions. But I never break! Really, never. I never give in. They can't imagine. They try, day after day, to be like me. That's the irony. Of course, they don't admit it, but they are constantly fighting their own battles against the biscuits. It's what we are told to do. It's what we should all be doing. I am just doing it to a further degree.

I will stop this when I am ready. I don't know how, because I don't really think in that direction at the moment, but I am sure there will be a way out when I am ready. They think I am like other girls and boys who have eating problems, but I don't see myself like them. I didn't realize it was such a big thing. I had no idea about anorexia before this or even what it meant. I never aspired to it. I never thought about it before. It is not like I wanted to join this club. Anyway, I am carrying on as normal because I can. Everyone seems surprised. But I have to carry on as normal because that is what I know. This is tiring. Thought is tiring. It is easier to just keep going forward, bit by bit. And to eat my medium-sized tomato to fill me up in the afternoon.

And so the scenario goes something like this.

Dr Whitecoat: 'How about it if Dad were to make you some cottage cheese on crackers before you go to bed?'

I shrug my shoulders and force a reply. 'I can't.'

Mum starts to cry.

Now Dr Whitecoat has made my mum cry and this makes me feel so sick.

'I can feed myself . . . you don't understand . . . I'm not a child.'

I hardly consent to the words; I don't like talking to him because then he thinks I am playing along. I hardly move my tongue. I force it back into my throat so that the words get stuck on my lips. My mouth hardly moves.

Dr Whitecoat shifts and smirks. 'You realize that you won't be going anywhere if you don't get better. To tell the truth,

I highly doubt that you will get to university this time next year. And to think of applying to Cambridge, that is surely the worst decision! Have you thought of going to a college closer to home? Then you could continue to come here and Mum and Dad could keep an eye on you.'

Bang. Bang. Bang. Degrading, disgusting doctor, white-coat. He makes me explode.

'I'm not staying in this fucking shithole and I'm sick of your fucking interference. I can sort this out myself. It is so demeaning to sit here while you talk about fucking cottage cheese . . .'

I stop myself. Who cares about cottage cheese? They think they know my patterns so well that now they are trying to adopt them for themselves. They are trying to talk in my anorexia language. They really have no idea.

Their other tactician is the nice-lady-dietician. She tries a different approach. Dr Whitecoat isn't very popular, and he only talks about the feelings side of things, whereas nice-lady-dietician is supposed to get to the nitty-gritty of the food business. So this time, it is another hospital and another corridor with brown plastic seats and old ladies. Nice-lady-dietician is a mother; she talks of her two children (who haven't wrecked their families and who do eat their Christmas dinner) and their successes. Her daughter, who I went to school with (but we don't mention that), is at university, and she is studying to be a doctor. She is lovely and jolly, and probably fatter than me and very happy. I am glad for the nice-lady-dietician's jolly daughter, but I am very pleased that I don't have to eat the nice-lady-dietician's dinners. I have to sit on some scales, which look like a big potty, and the whole place smells of wee. I can see why they are doing this to me. They want to degrade me. Perhaps they think that if they sit me here like a baby or an old person, I will feel humiliated into eating. It only makes me feel sick and cold and dirty. I want to get out of my clothes and lie in a boiling hot bath and forget this. I let them do it, only so I can be left alone.

I have made some pretty patterns in my food diary. I have to write down everything I eat and drink. This must include all things such as laxatives (I don't use these – I am not even sure what they look like – but I wonder if I should). No one believes me when I say it anyway. The nice-lady-dietician is, of course, impressed by the accuracy of my diary. Amazingly, I have managed to do this most difficult of tasks. It feels like school in a boring, easy lesson with a patronizing teacher.

'Well done, you,' she says.

I have correctly charted each hour of the week with perfect regularity. I have used the blank page very creatively to make her happy. I don't like to disappoint. Give me a new challenge and I will rise to the occasion. My diary looks like this:

Monday	*9 a.m.*	*Special K with semi-skimmed milk and a glass of hot water*
	10 a.m.	*water*
	11 a.m.	*Diet Coke*
	12 p.m.	*large apple*
	1 p.m.	*soup*
	1.15 p.m.	*yoghurt*
	4 p.m.	*apple*
	5 p.m.	*Diet Coke*
	6.15 p.m.	*soup and slice of bread*
	6.30 p.m.	*yoghurt*
	7 p.m.	*water*
Tuesday	*9 a.m.*	*Special K with semi-skimmed milk and a glass of hot water*

10 a.m.	*water*
11 a.m.	*Diet Coke*
12 p.m.	*tomato*
1 p.m.	*soup*
1.15 p.m.	*yoghurt*
4 p.m.	*apple*
5 p.m.	*Diet Coke*
6.15 p.m.	*large soup and two slices of bread*
6.30 p.m.	*yoghurt*
7 p.m.	*water*

etc., etc., bla bla bla . . .

I don't mention that the bread is low calorie, or that the soup has only forty calories, or that I water down my skimmed milk. I add in 'two' slices of bread to help her think that I am progressing. She likes that. The nice-lady-dietician takes it all in. I think she believes me. I can't quite understand how she can. She has given me room on these pages on which to write myself some further time to get away from her. I want to keep this space as my own, and so on it I will create another world. I love writing and making nice patterns with words, so it suits me fine to create these lists for her. I lie to keep her out. I don't want her participation, thank you very much. I let her think she is participating, because otherwise she might become the not-so-nice-lady-dietician and that wouldn't be nice at all.

To be honest, it feels like I am wasting her time. I know she has been busy looking me up in her textbook to try and figure me out, but she isn't going to get me that way. It feels like she is playing a different game from the one I am in. She makes lots of suggestions about the things that I should be eating. She has made her own plans and patterns before our meetings and she talks me through them. Sometimes her suggestions are just ridiculous. Once she even mentioned cheese. She told me about the protein and calcium that comes from cheese.

'You need it for your bones.'

'You need it to be strong.'

'You need calcium to stop you from getting osteoporosis.'

But I don't care about calcium; I care about calories. She puts so much work into planning my every mouthful, I feel almost sorry to ruin her plans, but I think my patterns are much more feasible. I nod at her suggestions, and sometimes I think I might even try one of them, just for her. She starts writing in my book. I grit my teeth. I made it look so perfect, neat and aligned, and she scribbles in pencil about full-fat milk and eggs and horrible, impossible big, fat things. I want to rub out her pencil and make it look smart again. She senses my anger and asks if I am OK. I tell her that the eggs and cheese aren't going to be possible. She looks disappointed and scrambles for something to say. She looks sad. I don't like it when she looks sad, because it means that she thinks that I am sad. I am not sad. I am taking this all in my stride. I am still striding with some confidence.

'What about some energy drinks? Maybe you will find it easier to take in the calories that way – in a liquid form. Your calorie intake is dangerously low. You are eating less than a child on a starvation diet.'

It sounds to me like things are being accomplished. What am I to say? I don't want to refuse her. I don't want to make her feel even sadder; she might feel that she isn't doing a good job.

'OK then.'

She looks visibly relieved and starts searching for a prescription pad. She can go home now and tick me off her 'To Do' list. See how easy that was. She seems better already. She sends me off to the chemist. I queue like a good girl and when I get to the front I politely ask the pharmacist for the drinks. She walks back into her medicine cupboard and comes back to the window. She hands me a huge brown paper bag. It takes both my arms to carry it. I jolt. As I walk down the long hospital corridor, I tear the bag open and pull out the insides. I immediately turn over the silver packs to see the calorie value. One drink contains more than my whole day's allowance. The nice-lady-dietician doesn't get it. I don't follow orders like that. She can't impose such things on my carefully constructed plans. I don't eat sugar, glucose, energy – however they try to disguise it – and I certainly don't drink it. I am shaking with panic at the thought of putting these things inside me. I walk out of the hospital, wrap the drinks back into the brown paper bag and throw it in the bin at the bus stop. I keep a couple of packets to show to Mum, and I have to take a few horrible sips when I get home to show her that I am doing better, then I quickly pour the rest of it down the bathroom sink.

When they weigh me at the hospital, they do it very precisely. Almost too precisely. They have old-fashioned scales with weights, which need to balance out to give you an exact measurement. My scales at home are under my mum and dad's bed. They are often dusty and the indicator part doesn't always sit exactly on 0. I weigh myself in stones and pounds, but at the hospital they weigh me in kilograms. I spend ages trying to convert it from kilos to pounds into stones in my head while answering the doctor's questions at the same time. I am doing sums over and over in my head while they are talking to me about the latest threat to my well-being. Stones and pounds are better, I think. I have always measured it that way, since I was little, so I get a better impression of where I am relative to where I was a few years/days/hours ago. They tell me not to weigh myself, or at least to cut down on the amount of time I spend on the scales. I weigh myself lots of times in one day and some-times, if I get panicky, I weigh myself lots of times in one hour, or one minute. I don't let Mum and Dad know about the scales because I think they would get angry, so I have to tiptoe around the room and try not to make a noise when I get them out. I don't know if they know that I am doing it, but I am pretty good at hiding it. If I hear the slightest noise I am quick to get myself in front of the mirror and pretend I am brushing my hair. They haven't caught me yet. At the moment, the numbers on the scales don't ever go up, in fact, mostly they go down, so now I am below six stone. I wanted to get to six stone so badly. It was a target for a long time. It sounds so much better than seven. And miles away from eight. I can't believe I was eight. I don't want to get back near to seven because that is too close to eight, and when I got above eight that is when it all started to go wrong with the fat feelings and all this began. And I know how quickly it could happen. Just a few more calo-ries and my body might go into some kind of state of shock and then, there I am again, back up the ladder. Yes, I think it is important to keep weighing.

When I weigh myself at home, I always make sure I go to the toilet first to get rid of any water build-up, and I undress, so I can get an accurate reading. If I go to the hospital I do the opposite. I pile on my clothes and I drink lots to make them think that I am trying hard. They don't fall for this often and make me take off the layers, which feels like a bit of an exposure. I am the bad girl who is breaking the rules.

The worst thing is when I am on the scales at home and the phone rings. I can't ignore it, because whoever it is that is calling me will think I have collapsed or fainted (I haven't yet). So I pick up, then I hear the loving voice that breaks up at the other end before I have had a chance to tell them, 'I'm fine. Everything is . . .'

'We are so proud of you, we only want you to get well, nothing else. And your mum and dad love you so much – you are trying, aren't you? We know you are trying.'

Or, 'Just give the psychiatrist a chance – pretend he's a filing cabinet or a Dictaphone. Persevere with the help. Do it for me. You would make me feel happy if I knew you were doing all right, and concentrating on getting better.'

I gulp and grit my teeth. They are always like this – swamping me with love and tears and well wishes. All I can think about is the scales.

'Yes, yes, yes.'

I tell them nice things about my day to distract them. I need to make sure things are still on track.

Ten

My friend, I know you think things are bad. I can see it in your face. I can see how you look at me with horror and gasps and you just can't stop staring. I let it go, I can't let it interfere. And to be honest, why don't you pick up some magazines and reassure yourself? I do it all the time. They tell me all I want to know and more. I can spend hours analysing the thickness of one celebrity's thigh against another's. Mostly, now, I am not interested in the other contents of the magazine; I just want to know if I am getting to be anything like those skinny women. I scan the pages ferociously, lapping up the information. They talk about which diets they have tried, and their exercise regimes. I am an expert on this. Pick a celebrity woman and I will know what she does and doesn't eat, and which parts of her body she does and doesn't like. I don't really use their diets because they suggest eating too much food. I have my own, anyway. But I do like staring at them, for hours, trying to find some imperfections. It is sometimes easier to see their real shapes on the TV. I know that in the magazines they have been cut round and evened out, to make them even more dimensionless. Still, it is hard to imagine them as normal, with bulky shapes and lines like I have, when you see them like that − seamless, smooth, toned, refined. Perfected.

OK, so sometimes getting up quickly is a problem. I fall on the floor with a dizzy head and things go black, but I haven't passed out yet (not properly) so I think it means that I am still fine. When you come round to see me, it takes me a while to get to the door, but I make it, don't I? You seem very quiet when you say hello. I think you have come back from university just to see me, which makes me feel like I am ruining your weekend. I would like to stay in the house with my hot-water bottle, but you would find that boring, so we decide to go into town. You are laughing and I am trying to keep up with you. You walk so fast and you talk so much that there is scarcely time to breathe. You are a student now and you seem different, more confident. You talk a lot about drinking and new friends, bars, clubs and places that I don't know, and my legs are hurting and I am so tired. I don't make a fuss though, do I? I don't tell you about the pain, and I don't spoil your day. I just walk round the shops with a fuzzy head. I will make it back to the car, and I will feel fine. You don't talk to me about my not-eating thing. I think it makes you uncomfortable, and I am glad that you don't bring it up, because everybody else is always asking and interfering. I wish you were here more often because you are kind to me. Instead, you write me letters, which are funny, and it reminds me of school days, before the summer, before things went wrong. You always seem to sign them off with something worried and upset though.

Dear Grace,
    University is fun. I met this really cool boy. We got really drunk . . .
PS – please try not to lose any more weight.
    Lots and lots of love, take care of yourself. xx

Or there are the letters which spell it out loud (when you feel braver), and they make me feel guilty because I have upset you and given you something to worry about, when you should be having fun.

I don't look at you and see a normal person. This will sound weird, but when I saw you I was so shocked, you look dreadful and you know it.

It may be hard but you must try putting on weight, not just staying the same. Those girls I saw on that TV programme about anorexia look hideous. If you keep losing weight, you will end up like them.

I wish you wouldn't bring it up; it is honestly better not to talk in that way. I like getting your letters but sometimes they make me cry. I don't like telling people that I cry, but I do. Actually, your letters always make me cry. I cry a lot these days. But sometimes I haven't got the energy, and it seems to take less energy to shut down, be silent and not let out any tears.

It is strange watching you eat the cream cake. I buy a Diet Coke and you eat a cream cake. Do you often do that, I wonder? I can't help but count up the calories and grams of fat you take in, and I am pleased. I find the smells in the bakery very strong. I can taste the smell of the sausage rolls and pastry and cakes and buns and bread and things I don't eat. I wouldn't eat anything from that shop. I am glad you do, although I wonder if you are just doing it for me. Are you?

I make sure I have a hot bath when I get home. I need to try and get rid of all the food I have put inside me, and when you are in a hot bath it feels as though you are steaming it out. I even bought some Epsom salts because I read in a magazine that they are good for detoxifying. The woman in Boots looked at me in a funny way. I almost didn't buy them because of her funny look, but then I thought of my freshly stretched-marked skin and I decided it might help if I scrub away at it. I like to have lots of baths in one day. My family think that this is strange. It's just a bath. I want to be clean. I don't relax in there. Baths are my quick fixes. My back hurts, anyway, against the cold plastic and my veins pop out of my red skin. I like to put my head under the water because it feels like I am weightless. I can forget things for a second. Only a second, though, but a second is a long time for me.

Dr Whitecoat wants to know how it went with nice-lady-dietician. I feign some interest in the conversation. I tell him that the drinks are sickly and sugary, but I don't tell him that I put them all in the bin. I think he would actually be angry with me for that. So we talk about some mindless issues and he seems to be frustrated. He starts to tell me about what will happen when I get admitted into hospital. I will have a drip and tubes put down my throat so, 'You'd better start changing.'

If I drop below 35 kilos then he will have to 'section' me. He sighs loudly to my silence, and tuts.

I grin. I don't know why I grin but I do. I almost laugh, right out loud. He makes me giggle inside. He patronizes me in silly ways, so I try and shock him.

'I'm getting better, that just won't happen. I've submitted some of my essays – my best writing work – to Cambridge, so I will just have to wait and see if I get the interview.'

I steer the conversation off course. But he repeats, as if I didn't hear the first time: 'If you drop one more kilogram, if you drop to 35 kilos, then I will put this order on you, then you will be forced to come in here.'

He is on the back foot; he has only one response. I won't let him win. I will have to change my tactics. I won't be forced in there, like I am being punished. I wonder if he actually thinks he is an opponent in my game! He doesn't realize that I gave up challenging him weeks ago. Maybe he knows what I am doing with my avoidances and fobbing chitchat. I wonder if he thinks that by making me angry with him, I will use the anger to start eating. This won't work. He doesn't sit in my head for that long. He is only with me during the time that I sit in his office and I feel sick and degraded and stupid. I can't afford for him to take me over like that, to have more time with me.

I have decided that I have to get out of his poky room where I sit once a week in silence and then go home and carry on as normal. My current strategy can only really last so long before someone finds out that it isn't working. I will have to make someone do something else, before they move me in to this old, whitecoated hospital.

'One hour a week. It's just not helping and he's not helping – we sit in silence most of the time, it's pointless – I need something else,' I tell Mum.

I look up at her as she gives me a hug.

I avoid Dr Whitecoat for a couple of weeks. He doesn't have much space in his busy diary and I am pleased to know that he is taking a Christmas break. This means I can stall him. I will try my hardest not to see him again.

Eleven

Mummy, Mummy, I need you. I woke up in the dark middle of the night and I screamed because I thought I saw a mouse in the bedroom. I thought I saw it run across the floor. I am sorry to wake you up. I have bad dreams. They make me cry. I can't cope. I can't cope with the bad dreams. I see people standing by my bed and I can hear people trying to come in and get me. I need you, Mummy. I don't want to sleep in my own room. I can't sleep any more. I wake up all the time and things hurt and I feel so so so cold like I am going to freeze. I have got layers of blankets and hot-water bottles and I am sleeping in my socks and jumpers but I just can't seem to get warm. Help me, Mummy.

Look at my arms. You can see my bones and these big blue veins popping out of my skin. I can't breathe any more because I am crying so much that I get all tight in my chest. I am not sure this will ever end. Some nights I have been thinking what it must be like to be able to eat McDonald's or pizza. Maybe one day I will, Mummy, maybe one day I will get better and be able to eat anything you want me to, but for the moment I can't. I can't because I am scared. I am scared of not being able to stop. Things would get so out of hand and I can't imagine having to feel the horrible fat feelings I used to have. It makes me feel ill. Do you remember how I ordered takeaway pizza on my eighteenth birthday and I drank champagne? I can't believe I did that. Was it really me? Then I sit and think about it, about how I used to be able to pick up the fat bits of my body, and I am so scared. I can't see the doctor again. I don't like him. Maybe you don't like him too? There must be some other things I could do, Mummy, to get better for you. Maybe we could see if we could find another doctor. I will try if it makes you feel better. I will come with you and visit some places if you want, and I will make an effort this time, I promise. Just don't make me go back and see Dr Whitecoat.

Mummy, thank you for taking me to the private hospital with the nice nurses who smile and don't shout, and who don't ask me intrusive questions. It reminds me of a posh hotel with clean sheets and TVs with satellite channels and cosy towels. I think it would be nicer here than on the sofa at home, wouldn't it, Mummy? It would be a nice change of scenery here. I think I would like it if it was all clean and nice, and people brought me things and looked after me. I am smiling, Mummy. I am smiling at the nurses. Does that make you happy? I know I have let you down, so I will try and make it better. I will try and sit on the bed in the room and let expensive doctors talk to me. If you want, Mummy. I don't think you do, though. I don't think you really want me to come here and let the expensive doctors take all your money. Money that you don't even have. So it would probably be better, wouldn't it, Mummy, if I just stay at home and we look for something else? Thank you for taking me, though, and thank you to the nice pleasant nurse with the smart blue uniform and the very pleasant hospital room. Perhaps we can look somewhere else – somewhere that is just for those with eating disorders. I haven't met any people like me properly yet. I find myself staring at them if I come across them in the street, and I have read their books, but I haven't met a real live one yet, a real live bulimic, anorexic or overeating person, and maybe it will help me if I did that. Maybe I will be able to make some friends or relate to their problems or something. That's what they say, isn't it, Mummy,

that it helps to meet people who are like you because you
have things in common and you can make sense of it together?

So we are discussing it, and then suddenly we are all there,
you, me and Dad, just like it was on that horrible day at
the doctor's surgery. We are in a big, empty house with high
ceilings and white walls and I feel like I have been trans-
ported out of my world into someone else's. I sit next to
you on a sofa and a nurse makes you and Dad cheese sandwiches. I eat my WeightWatchers' yoghurt. We make some
brief chitchat. She shows us the kitchen. It is colourful and
there are lots of charts and pictures on the walls. You stand
and talk to the nurse while I am introduced to two of the
girls who live there. They take me into the garden and tell
me what fun it would be if I moved in. They talk about
how they have pizza nights and how although it is difficult,
'It's a good place to be.'
    Then I am back in the kitchen, and I can see one of the
girls making a list of foods that she wants to eat over the
next week. A woman sits with her and tells her that she must
add in some toffee pudding and some custard to her menu.
    'If you have tomatoes for lunch, then when are you going
to have the pudding? Do you think you can manage it on
Tuesday, or do you want to have it on Wednesday instead?'
The nurse holds her pen over the paper on which she is
writing and lifts her eyes to the skinny girl, awaiting a
response.
    Then I am in a bedroom and there are photos of a girl
on the wardrobe. It looks nothing like the girl who is talking to me, but it is the same person.
    'And this would be your room. Claire stays here but she
has been discharged so it will be good to have someone else
in the house. Claire has got better. She still comes in though,
as an outpatient.'

She looks me up and down. The girls make me feel sick. I can't look at them. They look disgusting. All the food talk is making me feel so bored.

'What are you scared of eating?' they ask me. 'We all have something.'

I tell them it is cheese. I don't know. All I can hear is my inside voice shouting at me in a siren-sound, *No way, no way. No way. Get out, get out, get out.*

'Thank you, thank you so much for showing me round. Thank you. Bye-bye.'

'See you soon,' they reply.

No way, get me out, get me out, get me out.

I walk to the car and smile. I put my seat belt on and eat my apple. Have I done OK? It is later than I usually eat my apple so I feel a bit shaky. Dad looks pleased with me. He turns round and smiles at me sitting in the back seat.

'What did you think?' he asks me.

It's just an apple. Big deal – what's the fuss about?

Fifty-five calories and counting . . .

A letter

Daddy Dear Dad,
I don't know how to start this.

I sit on my bed and I shut the curtains. I take my hot-water bottle out of the cover and replace the roasting rubber-smelling pink heater against my red skin. I pull up the duvet covering my knees and I bring it up to my chin. I put down my notepad and reach for my glass of hot water from the bedside table. I press my fingers against the steamy mug. Anything for heat, things are cold these days. Then I take up my notepad and start again:

This letter will not reach you, Dad, but I will write it anyway. Dad, I don't know what to do. But I can't go to that place. It was so kind of you to drive me all the way there. You have always put me first, haven't you? But now I just need my own duvet and my own hot-water bottle and the smell of my home near me. And I don't want to go to that big, old, cold empty house. You don't want me to go either, do you? I know you don't, because when you ate your cheese sandwich in brown bread with butter and drank your tea with milk and ate two dark-chocolate-covered digestive biscuits that the nurse lady gave to you, you looked sort of uncomfortable. The nurses were trying to talk to you and you were nodding along, but you were probably thinking about all the pounds I was going to cost you and about all the loans and the debts that you would have as a result of me. I know you have always said, 'Grace, if you end up working on the cash tills in Woolworths and you are happy, then I'll be happy.'

If I told you it wouldn't make me happy to be in that cold house with the girls (who look nothing like their photos), then I think you wouldn't want me to go.

It's not for me, Dad. I'm not like them. I don't want to be like them. I didn't do this to get the label. I did this to sort myself out, I think. I just needed some time. I didn't become ill to make friends with other people who were doing the same thing. I know everybody thinks that, but no no no no.

Thanks, Dad. Sorry.

Grace

Dad gets a letter from the cold house. They offer him a half-price discount for me, but I don't want to go there. I promise him that I will change. I will. I promise. I am not going there, or anywhere like it, not ever. I am not one of those girls. I promise. I will make things better for them all.

Twelve

Then, there it is, a letter on the doormat, asking me to come for an interview at Cambridge University. There will be no calorie counters and wall charts and no toffee pudding if I don't want it. Of course, nobody is really happy for me. They would like to be, I am sure, because they are always proud of me, but instead they look at me and then they feign a smile while thinking, 'You're not going anywhere.' I know what they think.

They let me go on the train on my own to Cambridge, well thank you so much. I am nineteen. I could have a job, or children, or be married, so thank you so much for letting me go on the train on my own.

It's cold and dark in Cambridge and I haven't eaten all day because the train has upset my routine. I am quite nervous, anyway, so I think it is best not to eat at all. But now I have churning tummy pain – big, wide, stretching pains which are full of nothingness. It feels like my stomach is screwing itself up. There is no cottage cheese here, and I can't see any sign of a shop which is open near the college. I stand in my temporary Cambridge room and try and imagine it as my real one. There is no carpet and so I sit on the bed shivering. I can't get the pains out of me, so I decide I have to find some food. There is a pub near the entrance where I came in, so I walk over there on my own. I am not used to going out. I am sure people are staring. There is a bar and lots of people laughing. The barman smiles at me. Suddenly I order a Diet Coke and a jacket potato with tuna mayonnaise. I almost don't mean to say it; it just falls out my mouth. It arrives on a plate bigger than I can ever remember eating from. The tastes are so strong – the creamy mayonnaise is thick and gloopy and the jacket potato is boiling hot. I can feel the hot stuff moving inside me through my throat, and then my chest, and down into my stomach. My stomach makes confused noises and the pain is digging. The barman keeps watching me. He must know. He comes over and makes small talk. I want him to shut-up-and-leave-me-alone. Maybe he is attractive? I have no idea. I don't think about that any more. Not at all. He tells me that they serve lunch too. I wonder if he can tell. He must be able to tell. Thank you, no thank you. One jacket potato will keep me going for a long time.

I can't sleep in the cold, hard room. I read my notes and reread them. I toss and turn. I need the toilet, but am too scared to go down the stone steps to find one. There are some boys playing music. I don't know them and I don't want them to see me or hear me or even know I exist. I set the alarm early because I need to get up to do my exercises, especially after the jacket potato. So I get up at 5 a.m. and do my press-ups on the hard concrete floor.

In the morning I go to the breakfast hall. I stand in a long line of people with trays full of eggs and beans and toast and cereal and sausages – for breakfast! My eyes dart around the room looking for something I can manage. I am relieved to see a diet yoghurt and an apple. I sit down in the hall at the end of a long table, but I don't want to talk to anyone so I don't make eye contact or smile. I finish quickly and walk away leaving the others to their second helpings.

I don't like the other candidates in the waiting room because they are all focused and nervous. I am convinced they must be better than me, trained by their schools and their parents for success, so I am glad when the interviewers call me into the interview room, which has a real fire. I am happy about the fire because of the cold inside me. I am also glad that the interviewers are men. I don't think they even notice that I look different, and I have put on lots of layers so it is harder to tell. It hurts my back and my bottom sitting in the interview, everything is hard and unforgiving. I answer the questions, but I know that I could do better. When I am this cold and this stiff I can't seem to reach for things to say. The men are very friendly and they don't really ask me anything difficult, which is nice of them. They read my essays and they liked them. They liked my writing, so I like them.

'What kind of thing do you do socially?'

I tell them I love acting. I love being on stage. They smile at me. Do they know? Did someone tell them?

I have a new best friend now. Somebody who picks me up in her car and takes me to the pub. (I am not allowed to drive because doctors and families and friends say that I am too weak. I disagree. I am strong.) My friend is bored too; she has taken a year off from university and so she is pleased that she has got me for company. She doesn't make a fuss about my eating situation. In fact, she tells me that she always feels fat. It makes me a bit jealous and I worry that she isn't eating enough, but at least I don't think I'm such a failure. She seems to eat OK when I see her, so that makes me feel better. I am glad she takes me to the pub. It makes me seem more normal. I have got someone to drink my Diet Cokes with. The only thing that bothers me is the noise. All the people in the pub shout and scream above each other. They have so much energy, they make jokes, they laugh too loudly and I have to join in. It hurts my head and I feel drowned. Sometimes the drowning helps, because it means that I have some head space when I am not thinking about the next thing I have to eat. I get down to 95 per cent food thoughts, and the 5 per cent relief is like a cool slither of air. I still get excited when my friend tells me she is taking me home because I can think about being able to eat my afternoon snack, which makes me calmer. The pub is freezing and my mouth is too cold to speak.

Sometimes we drive around because my friend gets bored sitting in the same place all day. We pick up another girl and they sit in the front playing their favourite music loud, singing and laughing along, and it hurts my ears. I can hear better since I stopped eating; it is amplified, so the music makes me want to be sick. I am cold in the back of the car and I don't want to open my mouth in case some heat escapes. I pack myself up by folding my arms under my armpits and pulling my knees up to my chin. I feel like a tight ball of ice as I huddle in the back, waiting until I am taken home. I don't want to tell anyone that I am feeling like this. They will only shut me away in a room and I will have lost. It is better to be out. I don't like to lounge around all day as if I am sad.

I go to my friend's house most days too, just to get some space and to get some air. Her family are grown-up, they sit around chatting and drinking wine. Today they had smoked salmon on brown bread with butter (little triangles arranged beautifully on big, white, solid plates). I ate several little triangles. All my rules were broken; snapped in two. I have never eaten smoked salmon before because mostly, in my family, we have traditional northern food, or we have frozen meals, not things like smoked salmon. I don't know why I am able to eat the smoked salmon; I can't explain it. I wouldn't eat it at home. I won't feel good tomorrow, I will wake up in a panic and I will keep running to the scales, but I let myself, just this once, without knowing why.

I need to get away like that. Away from my family, who sit on the sofas every Friday night and eat newspaper-wrapped fish and chips and mushy peas and cans of full-fat Pepsi. All I can think about when they do that is about how I want to break out of it, break out of the growing-up house. All I want is to find my own space, go to Cambridge and be a success. I grind my teeth and I pull a face and I think about how I should be somewhere else. This isn't right any more. I don't know where that came from; where this longing grew up, but I know I have always felt different from everyone else, eating their fish and chips on the sofas.

I have to go to my best friend's birthday party at a pizza restaurant. I haven't been to a party in a while. I haven't been to a restaurant either. People round the table watch me – staring at my plate, my mouth, my fork and at my reactions. They are shocked that I know how to eat, but of course I do! It's just that usually I eat on my own so they don't see me do it. I don't like being watched. They eat pizza and drink wine and I have salad. I have a huge salad with beans and mayonnaise and pasta. As I take in every mouthful I try to work out the calories in my head. Usually I have all the labels in front of me, but here there is nothing, no information. I am glad I didn't eat anything else today. I finish my plate and I feel like there is a huge hole. I don't know if I feel full, empty or hungry. I just can't believe I have come to the end of the plate. I start to panic. I think I need more. I think I want more. I knew that this would happen. So I go to the salad bar and I get some more. People look at me. They tell me, 'Your salad looks so appetizing.'

They actually want to try some. All of sudden, there are other people's forks in my salad and they are commenting on it and eating the best bits. Maybe they are trying to make things normal but I want them to get back to eating their own doughy-smelling pizza.

Eat your pizza, leave me alone.

I sit perfectly still while they eat their desserts. I wish I had the strength and power to throw it all up.

Perception

I can barely see my anorexic self in my head now. I look inside my memories for clues as to how I then appeared to the outside world. All I can see are people's dropped mouths and uncomfortable faces looking back at me, around a pizza restaurant table, in a clothes shop, on the street, trying to conceal their true feelings. I can imagine the shape they saw, hauntingly thin, drawn, hollow – certainly not the same shape I perceived myself. I try to figure out how I saw my body – what it really looked like to me, how it appeared to me then. There are few photos of me at the worst time – at the lowest weight. Like my feelings, which have been whitewashed out of my memory, the brutal photos have been destroyed, as if no one wanted to admit me to any part of history.

Such a different, and yet similar, body lies before me now. I walk along the edge of the sea on a windy summer's day. I look down and out at my shadow, which is outlined in the sand, blown up, distorted and fuzzy-edged. I pull my hands into my sides and my body becomes an amorphous mass, this black shape lying in front of me. I move my arms up and out to the sides, waving them in the air and my trunk is suddenly smaller, lesser, lighter, freer. My shadow shows up the object of me – I am there on a second substance, which is fickle, and as I turn, it moves. There is no light; there is no enlightenment here. There is only an insubstantial image, which moves with the water of the tide beneath my feet, and the wind, which blows my image into different shapes.

I stand in front of a mirrored bathroom cabinet, where the two doors of the cabinet meet. My body is reflected half in one side and half in the other. I look at the whole and it makes me shrink. I move my eyes from the shrunken image to the reality, shrunken image to reality and wonder just what the reality is. It is all about perception. The power of the mirror is only as strong as the person reflected in it.

When an anorexic looks in the mirror, her own form looks large, rounded and curved. Her eyes sharpen on the other bodies around her while her interpretation of her own image is skewed. Others see her as thin − skeletal − but she struggles to understand their perspective. Two sets of eyes see the size of the body completely differently. She fears her own shape − it becomes, like a monstrous creation, the seat of all discomfort, pain and anxiety, while the idea of an alternative, thinner shape provides comfort, stability and re-assurance. We translate our own shape and size through a myriad of other emotions and sensations internally, and end up with something removed from the starting point.

It is hard to understand this, and because it is hard to understand, there is not always sympathy for this plight. Some would say that anorexia is pure self-indulgence, anorexia is caused by vanity; she has been staring at her reflection for too long; surely she should try to pull down all the mirrors and stop being so self-absorbed.

'Just get on with it, love.'

Anorexics are disproportionately self-absorbed, there is no way to write about this illness without confronting that; it is where the illness takes them, only further inwards, as they reject the outside. The mirror actually means very little because the object that is seen in it is translated and altered depending on the mood on the inside. And that object − that body − is always hovering below her, as if it is a detached and separate entity, something which the mind must suppress.

Why else would she stare in the mirror a hundred times a day, checking the millimetres of fat on her thighs? Why else would she chastise herself for days on end for the three pieces of popcorn she ate before bed? The body is the enemy, it must be weakened and shrunk and suppressed. It is controllable, it is physical and alterable. Food equals fat and starvation equals thin. How can she live with herself if this less than perfect body actually *is* her self? The equation petrifies.

I continued to not-eat because what I perceived in the mirror image did not shock me like it seemed to shock other people. It didn't make me scared to see something so thin; it was more intriguing than anything else. I just observed it, almost like I would do with an animal in a zoo. I saw its movements and bony bits, and I didn't really relate them to any particular part of what I termed 'me'. I squashed the remaining flesh and I saw it as countering me because I didn't feel that it represented who I was. The fat didn't need to be there and I could do without it. I could be this image of myself in my head without any of this surface, surplus body.

I covered things up because people stared at me. I wore layers of clothes because I was so cold and frozen that I needed to wrap up. Layering also played another role; I felt ashamed that everyone thought I had failed. It was better to keep my head down, not be seen, not see anyone else and not be in anyone's photos of Christmas or New Year. The hair on my arms was getting thicker. My head hair was dropping out in clumps on to my hairbrush. I convinced myself that it was better to wear a hat, because of the cold escaping through my head. I always had ways of rationalizing my behaviour and logically explaining things away, especially what I saw as other people's flawed perceptions of my own body.

Achievement

As my weight continued to decrease and I became more and more shocking to look at, I continued to increase the amount of activity I was doing. I followed a semi-normal existence in terms of my day-to-day routine; I was shopping, talking, reading, studying, watching TV and exercising (of course). My breaking-down body was held up only by a tightly focused mind, which continued to try and hold up its own illusion. This ability to focus on achievement and studying is common to people suffering from anorexia.[13] It is hard to understand how someone who is not-eating, and is therefore in a starved state, can carry on with such intense activity. In one sense, it is a powerful distraction from thoughts of food and the intensely painful hunger which you crush, and in another, it is part of the bigger issue, that constant need to achieve intellectual aims, while ignoring the issue of emotional maturity.

Achievement had always been something central to my life. I did not want to let anyone down. I believed that I had made my family, teachers and friends happy by being good, strong and achieving things, and I wanted to continue with this (this was not necessarily their view of things, but my self-made one). I wanted to make them proud. Academically, I just wanted to get better. In my bettering, I believed there would be this happiness, which I had not yet found. I placed huge pressure upon myself to achieve everything I set my mind to, and the terror of the thought of failure was paralysing. In the end, my anorexia may well have been some

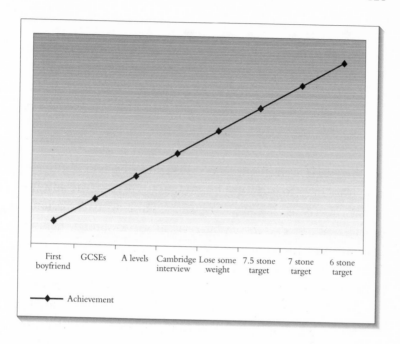

First boyfriend | GCSEs | A levels | Cambridge interview | Lose some weight | 7.5 stone target | 7 stone target | 6 stone target

◆— Achievement

sort of withdrawal from this conflict between the desperate need for success and the consuming fear of failure. Becoming anorexic was temporarily a break from the whole cycle.

The irony is that although I was focused on achieving academic, external things – I was hugely articulate when describing world affairs – when it came down to my own emotions or expressions of my feelings, it was as if I no longer had access to my own senses. Looking back, my senses seem numbed. My speech was constrained by what I felt I had to say so as not to upset anyone, my sight was in food-focused tunnel vision. I did not taste, I stopped the enjoyment of it and I laced it with guilt. Smell was the one sense that remained strong, and it became stronger as I stopped eating. Smells of bread and cake and fish and chips seemed to possess me. Amazing how the smell of the body spray I used at this time fills me with a sickness and sends a tremor through my body, immediately transporting me back.

Family and friends tried to ask what I felt; they tried to talk to me. They must have wondered why I didn't talk to them or ask for help and why I was so closed up. They stared at me as I sat on the sofa, playing with my salad. I was in a different place from them, somewhere else where things were 'absolutely fine'. I refused to respond to what my body was showing outwardly; instead I only listened to my internal drive. They were crying and not sleeping and not eating (most irritating to me), and pulling the hair out of their heads trying to think of ways to reach me, and I was just sitting there making notes on my books, making further plans to achieve.

As an anorexic, it is almost impossible to connect with those feelings everyone is desperate for you to express. The answer nearly always is: 'I'm not feeling anything. I'm just feeling fat, big, huge, yuk, flab, skin, lines, sick-making fat.'

There is a blockage. Fat is the only thing that is being felt. The aim of everything is always to get back control, to achieve and to be better, and feelings seem irrelevant to this. The cruel reality is, however, that in each self-bettering comes more self-battering. When doctors and friends and family told me to be still, to switch off, to relax and rest, I could not understand what it meant. I was anxious; there surely must be more I could achieve; there must be things I could do to be better – to be thinner – to be better.

Anxiety

Anorexia nervosa (of nervous origin) and anxiety by definition sit side by side. Anorexia fixes and controls (temporarily) anxiety – it provides a single focus for fear to be played out – and anxiety builds and feeds, grows and festers beneath the surface of the anorexia. Indeed, the issue of anxiety and its relation to problems of identity formation is often cited as a key factor for some people who suffer from anorexia.[14] Anxiety has prevented these individuals from experiencing and overcoming risk situations. As young children, something has inhibited them from being able to explore enough. They therefore have been unable to learn by experience; they have not faced up to their fears. As a result they fail to find a set of limits or edges, which define their sense of self[15] and so they try and forge a sense of identity through losing weight and changing their shape.

I was always an anxious child. I was never a free-flowing spirit who ran with every new and dangerous thing. I thought of every possibility in all action; that way I would not be disappointed or surprised. I preferred the limits of my imagination (which felt and sensed everything in extraordinary filmic detail) rather than the reality of a canoe or a rock climb or a fun fair. For other people, adrenalin came in the form of breaking the rules, taking a risk and playing with fortune. But that path offered nothing to me except terror. I was a first child, and always cautious. I was sure of my academic identity, but the shelter of my home environment and the sense of safety I grew up in perhaps did not allow me to fully develop a sense of edges for myself.

When it came to my anorexia, I was convinced that if I gained any weight, I would spiral out of control. I was not confident of my own limits. I was terrified of what was on the other side of weight gain and who I would become if that happened. But my fear of weight gain was not like any other fear I had known. It was not like my fear of dogs or dentists or strangers. It did not send my heart racing or make me sweat or shake. It sat deep inside me and it reverberated loud inside my head, a voice on repeat, repeat; a record stuck. I had become scared of eating, scared of what would happen with every mouthful, but at the same time I was fascinated by food. I did not cross the street to get away from it, like I did when I saw dogs or dentists or strangers; I walked towards it, and I stared at it. I lingered in front of shops and I hovered around its smells. It did not make me jump with anxiety like flying and roller coasters and heights, it made me salivate.

Could it have been that anorexia was a reaction to my anxious and fearful personality? Could it be that anorexia is in my genes? The genetic story is an impossible one to ignore and more and more research is heading this way.[16] There is evidence to suggest that there is a higher prevalence of eating disorders in families where relatives have suffered from anorexia or bulimia. This is some comfort, to think that you have not brought it upon yourself (as everyone is suggesting), but that it was going to happen to you, whatever you chose to do, or not to do – the anxiety, the anorexia, your personality . . . everything.

Outside v Inside

Anorexia has been described as having 'biopsychosocial' origins (its influences are genetic, psychological and socio-cultural ones).[17] Doctors and scientists and sociologists do not necessarily agree on how or why it starts – or where it grows from. We can therefore be confused into believing that eating disorders are all too mysterious and strange and that those who experience some form of them must necessarily be mysterious and strange too. Many people seem to be satisfied with such a flimsy conclusion; that eating disorders are everywhere, that an inexplicable plurality of factors causes them – culture, self-obsession, things that happen somewhere else to weird people. However, despite emerging evidence on the genetic front, many of these issues that are explored in a discussion on anorexia are societal ones, which affect and surround us all. That is the thing about anorexia; it uncomfortably reflects back society's ideals gone wrong, the misshapen view that perfection and happiness are obtainable through the body.

As an anorexic, the job of trying to imagine myself with a bigger, so-called healthier body, which everyone kept asking me to do, was made more difficult by the presence of the perfect, glossy images of the ideal body which surrounded me. (In 1996, there were far fewer celebrity-focused magazines than there are now, but it was still something that I was hugely aware of.) I thought that I couldn't be doing anything too bad because I still had bits of flesh, fat and curves where celebrities seemingly didn't. Even though they were thin like me, they were thick with gloss and shine and health. So how could I be so wrong?

I looked at the images and compared them to my mirror image. I stared hard at the outlines. I played spot the difference. I couldn't understand why people were telling me that I was going to die. How could my body be the object of all this attention and ever-increasing shouting, thumping pressure, when the pages of the magazines told me that I was emulating, and that I was emulating well? Explanations and revelations of the perfect and imperfect body were at my fingertips. Lots of pictures and images and words went in from the outside and I soaked them up. And the more I went inwards, the harder it was to look outwards and see what was meant by a 'normal' shape and a normal diet.

Anorexia nervosa is now joined by other similar body-based obsessions (some media-coined, others medically verified) related to the perfection of body shape: bulimia (bingeing and purging), yogarexia (an addiction to yoga),[18] orthorexia (an obsession with healthy eating)[19] and stress-orexia (serious over-exercise).[20] It is almost openly acceptable to have an out-of-balance relationship with food and exercise, to be addicted to thinking about it, to be eating food or not-eating it. All of these addictions form their own set of internally constructed rules. We equate our success with how much we weigh. The end result of these fixations must surely be that this denial and control actually become what we are about. When it comes to food control we can literally be aiming to reach nothing. In America, retailers have created a size specifically for the nothing-women: size zero. Perfect for those who want to equal nothing and to find, in this nothingness, something that they don't seem to find in their own flesh.

Commentators have argued that the seeming increase of

cases of eating disorders (particularly bulimia)[21] is linked to our society and to our obsession with thinness as a model of beauty. They might say that our perception of beauty and happiness is not one from the inside; it is not inherent, but is made up by our changing environment. Our society equates success with thinness; we are told that they go hand in hand; a successful woman is one who is shrinking. Flesh and fat are considered to be the anti-thesis of power, control and achievement. Often, a celebrity female's success is based on an image of persistence, of self-control and of willpower over her body. Could it therefore follow that the anorexic girl who cannot conceive because her periods have stopped, who has reverted out of womanhood, and who represents a sense of closure and isolation, is telling us that she has attained total perfection? She has blocked out to focus in.

There is much denial of the culpability of magazines and models and the media in 'causing' eating disorders. A direct causal link seems too strong to me. There is a distinction between those who follow a diet from a magazine and leave it at that, and those who develop an eating disorder. But when vulnerability and low self-esteem are exposed, media-generated idealizations of beauty surely further this insecurity and self-loathing. This obsession with the perfect body adds pressure and stimulus to the potential to turn the fight further inwards. The messages transmitted by some magazine editorials, by advertising and the fashion industry, are confusing. One minute it is, 'She's too fat.' The next, 'She's too thin.'

We are left wondering, always believing, hooked into an industry of perfection, which is never obtainable, because they are always changing the model we should be operating to.

In today's consumer culture, we have a choice as purchasers and we appear to have control of what we want. We live in an 'if only' society: if only I had a bigger flat, a nicer car, a new pair of shoes, bigger breasts, a slimmer body. We have somehow managed to convince ourselves that these things will solve unhappiness. And ultimately we have decided to fight this battle out of dissatisfaction on our own territory, on ourselves – travelling inside to the point of self-annihilation (as with anorexia) to find the answer instead of questioning the outside influences which might be making us feel and act this way.

Even with this understanding that anorexia reflects uncomfortable truths about our society's ideals and expectations, the fact remains that anorexia nervosa (although only having the definition/name since the late nineteenth century), can be traced back a long time before this. Before the emergence of the glossy magazine, before feminism and post-feminism, before the suffragettes, anorexia goes back to the late 1600s and to Richard Morton's description of a seeming case of the disorder in his *Treatise of Consumptions* in 1694.[22] The social context may have changed, the perfectionist culture may exacerbate it, but way before any fashion for the female waif, a self-starving illness was around. It has been around for a long time. The diagnosis and knowledge of the illness may have increased, but the underlying disorder remains the same.

For a sufferer and for the family trying to make sense of this illness it is hugely confusing. They are left picking up parts of some theories and discarding others according to their own particular experience. It is frustrating that, given the magnitude of the illness and its apparent omnipresence, all of this research and media debate and discussion have not found a satisfactory conclusion. It is as if we have been conditioned to think that it is absolutely impossible to do so. Perhaps it seems easier that way, because it allows anorexics to get on with what they do best (keep starving), families to avoid changing their embedded behaviours and society at large to keep theorizing and gossiping, but without really addressing the issue.

Categorizing

When writing down my experience of my eating disorder, it seems easy to make assumptions about other people's experiences, as if we all suffered the illness in the same way. I am aware that this is not the case. I cannot speak comprehensively for over a million people in this country. This labelling was something that I encountered myself as an anorexic, and it really angered me. I felt that the psychiatrists and the books I read wanted to box me up. They wanted to confine me within the conventions of what my illness supposedly represented. And I rejected them.

'I'm not like them,' I told myself. 'I am above them. Totally different. My illness is unique to me. In fact, I'm sure I do it better than other people do. This is my story. One person, one version, individual.'

In the fifteenth and sixteenth centuries, self-starvation was seen to be an indication of bewitchment ('subject to the malefic influence of witchcraft').[23] And, in a sense, this is what had seemingly happened to me – I was taken over. I was removed from any knowledge of myself. I was bewitched (fascinated) by this obsession and I was bewitching (fascinating) to look at. Perhaps this is why there is the sense that eating disorders are too mystifying to deal with; that they evade understanding. There is a feeling that those under this trance-like behaviour are somehow strange and at odds with normal conventions; eating is normal.

I wanted it to be mysterious too. I (like many others) didn't want to solve it, because with solving my problems would come a realization that it might be about normal issues and that I might have to deal with those. It might be shown to be about my desire to please people, or my fear of failing, or my lack of a sense of identity. It could be about the fear that I would not fit in at university, be accepted, pretty enough, clever enough or match up to my previous successes.

I liked to think of my case as unique, I liked to think of my illness as having its own terms, I liked to think it was because I had that habit of over-thinking things. I endlessly intellectualized this illness and tried to make it my own. But as much as I try to deny it, I hear my very words spoken by other people who have experienced an eating disorder; the same metaphors, the same order of the same words and thoughts and events, almost as if we have read the same script. It is as if we have been invaded by the same virus, which transforms our words and our thoughts so that we are simply mimicking it in our own separate bodies. It is a terrifying realization, to hear what you feel to be parts of your self, who you are and what you feel as an individual, literally recited by other people. Pretending that you are somehow a rare and special person is an ineffective message to other people. It only propels the myth that anorexia is something over there on the margins of society, which can be ignored. I don't think I am special just because I suffered from anorexia nervosa and I don't think it was caused as a result of me being special in the first place.

Words often used to describe the prevalence of anorexia nervosa are 'epidemic' and 'plague'. As exaggerated as they might sound, they are an accurate reflection of the way it manipulates and intrudes into every facet of a person. In 1873, 'anorexia nervosa' was given a name. Ernest Lasègue, one of those who laid claim to discovering the illness, said that he found that those he encountered with anorexia were so alike in form and behaviour that he was able to see the resemblance and make his diagnosis without hesitation.[24]

★

As I dropped below six stone, three months after diagnosis, things got to the point where something different had to be done. As with many anorexics, my illness reached a new level of physical seriousness. There had been some intervention, but at the same time I was still deteriorating – I had continued to make progress with my self-starving. I kept going because it was my intention to do so, and I firmly believed I could control and manipulate my single-minded intentions. It was true that as my body initially weakened and my muscles softened, I gained an immeasurable mental strength and focus, but eventually my body became so frail that it seemed to lose interest in its own cause, and it started to give up. At this level of severe weight loss, doctors can identify several physical symptoms of anorexia: low blood pressure, a slower pulse rate and a lower body temperature.[25] With this physical collapse, which threatened all faculties (continuing and prolonged starvation can lead to a loss of fertility, osteoporosis and heart, gastro and kidney problems), I watched myself give in to it.

As I had never wanted to be a failure at anything (good, better, best), I looked over the object of my body and I cried, because what I had controlled and perfected was now helpless, strengthless and shapeless. When people looked at me they could not recognize me. There was no one to recognize. But I had continued to say to the psychiatrist, 'How dare you deign to know me? Don't classify me, don't box me up along with the others. I am an A student, an A-plus student. I am above this condescension, this reduction of my personality into this thing you call anorexia. You don't even know me.'

And he didn't. And I didn't.

Because I had not fully grown up, because this illness had pulled me up from the roots, right in the middle of the time when I should have been carving out my own independence, I did not have an understanding of myself. I was like a blank sheet on which this illness had inscribed itself; child, teenager, anorexic, as if it was all I was and all I knew. And so shouting about how I was really something else was ineffective because I had not allowed that something else to happen, I had blocked it. I was an anorexic now and I was a girl again, in need of help.

PART 3

What Am I Now?

Thirteen

A control freak, obsessional, a perfectionist, I am all of these things and yet feel like none. If I am such a freak then maybe I should be put on show. A travelling show from a hundred years ago, where giants and dwarfs and fasting girls who defied the laws of nature, who appeared impossible, were gaped at by the public. They sat, a cage within a cage, aesthetic spectacles, awaiting the look, the flinch of horrified intrigue from the faces on the outside. I am not craving this strange attention; I am not seeking to be a focus. I want to stay in my own little world, my prison. Don't come near my house. My body is my temple. Everything I do is under my own power. Don't you see that? I'm just asking for some space. I feel claustrophobic, like the bodies around me are too close. I draw these lines around me and shut everything out. I shut you out. I close up my mouth and I am whole. Impenetrable. I feel too much of myself; I take up too much space.

What am I?

I can't cope with the idea of them taking control away from me – of them locking me up with a bunch of girls who have scary pizza nights and make wall charts of their tomato fascinations. But it is what they keep suggesting. What if those girls do it better than me? At least on my own I am in charge of myself and I don't try new methods to get thinner. I don't think I want to talk about it with other girls. It would make me too jealous. The thought of some of them much below my weight – oh, the competition! And what if they talked about things I haven't done, like laxatives or binge-eating or making themselves sick? I would *have* to try them. I know they would also be looking at me and measuring the size of my wrists and my tummy and my legs, because that is what I would do. I would feel like I am being spied on. I wouldn't be concentrating on the whitecoats, I would be thinking about the other girls. I get funny like that.

I wonder if I was allowed liposuction, then maybe I wouldn't be an anorexic. Then I would have thighs like a supermodel and everything would be OK. But the books tell me that it is not about the fat, it is about the feelings. The whitecoats keep asking me about the feelings and I keep wondering what they mean. When they ask, 'How are you?' I wonder what they really want me to say. Things are a bit snowy-blind at the moment and, to be honest, I am not sure I know what a feeling is or how to really describe it.

Mum says it is appalling that we have had to wait all this time to get specialist help (Dr Whitecoat is a regular psychiatrist, not a specific eating disorders one). Apparently I have been on a waiting list for three or four months for outpatient access to an eating disorders unit, and in this time I have been losing more and more weight, and this is not acceptable. This is what everyone says about me. Mum has now got a letter from a special unit at another local hospital, and there is a place for me to go and speak to a new lady doctor who is the expert on people like me. Apparently I am very lucky for this unit to be so close to my house, and for someone so specialized in this field to be available to me. Mum has been reading books and writing letters to people and campaigning for me. Dr Whitecoat isn't happy with Mum because he doesn't understand why she thinks I need to go somewhere special like that, when his general psychiatric department can cope very well, thank you. He thinks I might be avoiding things, and he doesn't understand why Mum thinks he isn't the best doctor for her best daughter. But I don't like Dr Whitecoat and his sarcastic voice and his cynicism. I can beat him.

Then I get the letter I have been waiting for, and no one is happy for me and there are heads in hands and slammed doors, but I feel like calling Dr Whitecoat up and shouting down the phone.

'HA. There you go. Someone believes in me. Ha. Do you want to know what it says?'

Dear Grace,
    We would like to make you an unconditional offer.
From Queens' College
Cambridge University.

I hold the letter in my hands and I read it over and over again. I call my friends who don't/can't mention my problems, and they tell me that I have done well. I didn't even try as hard as I usually would in the interview because I was tired (and maybe hungry) and I still did it. I still did exactly as I said I would.

See, I will be the best, I will prove you all wrong. I will go to Cambridge and I will get away from all the people who are trying to peer inside my head and feed me foods that I can't eat. People will be amazed when I say, 'I go to Cambridge University.'

They will say, 'Ooh. A girl like you, how smart, haven't you done well? You must be really clever.'

I think they will be impressed and they will understand me. This label will be much better than my current one. This is my aim.

★

When I get to see the new doctor in the new hospital, she is very friendly. I have to go with Mum and Dad because it's a family session where she will try and see if it's because of my background and things from my past that I have turned into an anorexic. Most of the questions go to Mum and Dad and I am there in the middle with my good-girl look and my ready-to-learn face on.

'Did she play with dolls?' the female psychiatrist glances towards Mum. I look at Mum while she answers for me. Is this to disempower me? I wonder. They talk back and forth about my body, my history, my feelings. I scarcely dare move. I don't want them to think that I am interrupting their nice conversation.

'You see, she has never been any trouble, we have never had any problems with her.'

I listen to Mum talk about my childhood. I didn't cry much as a baby. I did all my homework. I was very helpful looking after my brother and sisters. I was top of the class. I always did my best. They never had to worry. I got drunk a bit with my best friends (Dad had to take us home in his car, opening the car doors when one of us needed to be sick!). But I didn't take drugs, or shoplift, or get pregnant, or get in trouble.

'No, no, nothing like that.'

Dad nods along. He is targeted by the doctor's questions, he feels uncomfortable and he responds hesitantly, shifting in his seat.

Mum interrupts, 'He has never had to deal with anything like this before. This is probably the worst thing that has ever happened to him.'

Do you see what you have done? Do you? Do you see how you have made them pale and shaky? Don't you feel responsible for stopping them from sleeping at night? Do you feel bad? You should feel bad. You don't deserve to get better.

They finish talking and I conclude that this discussion has been most interesting. I don't usually tend to dwell on things from the past.

They want to test my body and check that my blood is still working OK. It is cold on the hospital bed. I don't like the way they poke the sterile needle into my arm. It takes several attempts to get the blood out. I have big veins which stick right out of my arm, so I can't understand why they can't just get what they need and let me put my top back on my shivering body. They give me a big plaster when they finish and I roll up my sleeve. I hope that people will look at my arm and see that there is something really wrong. I wonder what they will think. See, I'm not making it up. There is something properly wrong. They even put needles in me. I think about what it would be like to be in a hospital bed, and have people come and visit me and bring me get well cards and flowers. People wouldn't dare bring chocolates or grapes or anything, but we wouldn't mention it (people don't like to mention it now, it seems, not in a public way). I would just have more non-edible items in my room than the usual person, probably a room of non-edible flowers.

Now I go every week to the special eating disorders unit to see the nice lady doctor. It is part of a big hospital so I don't mind going there. I have to walk past Accident and Emergency, and wards where old people are staying, and the X-ray section. Maybe people will think I am visiting a sick friend or a new baby and no one will guess that I am heading towards the psychiatry unit. I always make a quick dash to get in there. Once I am in, I am not too worried as I am sure there are people with worse problems than me. I tell the receptionists that I am here for my two o'clock appointment. They smile at me and tell me to go and wait

in the cramped waiting room, where every seat is filled. I
try and work out what everybody is doing there, because
there is a lot of waiting and a lot of lateness.

Today I have read through every magazine in the room
cover to cover, drunk two cans of Diet Pepsi and chewed
through two packets of sugar-free gum. My back is stiff and
my tailbone aches from sitting down in one place for so
long. Every few minutes there are footsteps, which lead to
the room, and occasionally someone is taken away. I wish
someone would come and get me, weigh me and measure
me, so I could go home or go shopping or go to the pub.
After two hours of waiting I am apologetically jostled into
the doctor's office. My nice lady doctor blusters her excuses,
rummaging through the files. She is friendly and bouncy. I
try not to make her feel bad, so I smile and look at the
pictures of her husband and daughter as she frantically
searches through her paperwork. She thinks hard to
remember my name or my illness.

'We have had an emergency come in, I'm sorry but this
will have to be it for today . . . You are OK? . . . Great
. . . Make another appointment.'

I don't mind not talking, that is fine, and I would rather
she didn't weigh me because she will see that I have not
gone up, and that I have not been following her instruc-
tions, but I HATE HATE HATE her wasting my time. I
hate sitting in that small waiting room with strange pictures
of African wildlife on the walls and the low, neutral brown
coffee table, which has copies of obscure journals and travel
guides and pointless leaflets lying on it. I hate sitting there
with all the other people, squashed up. I hate the way people
stare at me as I take out one piece of chewing gum from
my mouth and replace it with another.

It is none of your business, staring people. Leave me alone.

I hate the way I can't get comfortable on the hard chairs

and the nervy feelings I have to sit with every time a person looks my way.

How can I do this all on my own?

I am obviously not the worst; there are people whose bodies are a much lower weight than mine, maybe a whole stone less; I am not as bad as them. There are girls in here who can't move or walk, who sit in wheelchairs, whose teeth and heart and bones are demolished from all the sicking up and not-eating for years. I have seen them from afar at the other end of the corridor, and walking through town, when they must have been let out for an hour; away from the horrible foods they are made to eat. It is sort of fascinating, I think, even for me – how they end up looking like that. Perhaps that is what other people think too. Maybe that is why they can't talk about it. Anorexia is a strange, secret thing and they can't begin to imagine how or why it is done.

I can't get another appointment with the nice lady doctor because she is all booked up, like a really good hairdresser or posh restaurant. I am free all the time; I don't have anything to do. I lie on my sofa day after day, and I sleep, and I don't eat. She can't see me for three weeks, not even for half an hour, and so I will keep dropping weight because I can. Even though I would like to make it better for Mum and Dad and for everybody, I don't quite know where to start.

When I do eventually go and see the nice lady doctor she seems to buy into my speech about 'really trying hard not to lose weight' and 'feeling scared' too. It's not that I don't try and mean what I say, it's just that I can't properly feel it. It's like I am on the stage, looking convincing and talking about the 'feeling' things, but then I walk off and I am fine, back into my control. I just block what I said. At least I do talk to her a bit more than to Dr Whitecoat because I don't want to appear rude to such a nice lady. I tell her about the way 'I can't switch off. I see and hear everything. I can't stop. There is no stillness.'

I know she is impressed by my articulateness, the fact that I still have a brain. She decides to tell me all about the damage I am doing to my body and the long-term repercussions. She tells me about the weakening of my bones and the way I am affecting my electrolyte balance, and how it isn't normal for me not to have periods for over a year, and how I might not be able to conceive in the future, and how I definitely can't have a boyfriend because I am not strong enough to cope. But I am nineteen and things are a bit out of focus, to be honest, and so instead of being scared by what she says I learn it, store it and think to myself, 'I should make sure I remember, just in case I am tested. I should be the expert on this.'

If I was honest, and not performing to make her happy, I might say to the nice lady doctor:

'Thank you for the books that you've given me. There are some interesting points, which I have noted on the possible causes of an eating disorder. I am glad to see I fit the mould. I am not so abnormal as one would imagine, although where I come from, people aren't used to such spectacles, and so they stare and comment which makes me feel rather uncomfortable. The books I have read about American high school girls and college students, or stories from girls at posh boarding schools, don't fit with me. It's like reading Judy Blume or *Malory Towers*, not like my normal life in Durham. Maybe in other places anorexics are common, but they aren't here, at least not visibly. Here, anything different at all is magnified and examined and whispered about.

'I have noted the diet plans to which you have referred me and I honestly don't think they are achievable. Do you realize that one of the diets actually suggests that I eat 1,000 calories in one day? Can you see that this is impossible and unimaginable? I eat 300 calories a day at the moment so this is a 233.3 per cent increase on my current level. Can you do your maths? Would you be able to increase the amount you ate by that amount every day, if I asked you to? I suspect you will tell me that it is different, and that you do not need to increase your intake. But I look at the list of foods, and I am afraid that they are not things I can currently ingest and certainly not all at once. Your strategy seems to be to make me eat as much as possible, as quickly as possible. Surely if I could do this, I would have done it by now? I know how to eat, I just can't, something inside me won't let me. You are very nice, and I like you and your Laura Ashley dresses and your cluttered office, but I am not sure you are understanding me. Your books with their diet plans might seem to offer quick solutions, and your probing questions about my childhood might provide you with the answers you are looking for, but they don't give me any. I have done the spider diagrams, the life maps and all the funny psycho-analytical exercises the books suggest, and I don't mind because I'm bored sitting on the sofa and it gives me something to fill my time. I find it interesting, the psychological side of things. I might study it one day.

'I understand what you are saying, and I suppose it adds up, but it doesn't match my version of things. It's like another colour, which is not on my rainbow. I can see the way this is going. Your plans don't match mine. Eventually we will fall out, you and I, because the scales will give me away. If I keep dropping in weight you will eventually admit me into your horrible hospital. And I will say, "I'm sorry, I can't come to your hospital because I'm going to Cambridge University to study English and to be the best and so, you see, it isn't possible. I have other plans."

'And you will laugh, "Ha ha – silly little girl, you can't

go anywhere. You are an anorexic and you are not allowed. We say so."

'Then there will be tears and disasters and unimaginable things.

'So it won't be like this for much longer. It is nearly New Year. I won't be here next year. No. I won't be doodling life plans and food diaries and chatting through my personal inside thoughts next year. I just can't let it go that way.'

I want to prove everyone wrong. I want to prove I'm right and get to Cambridge, and be on my own. There, I can escape other people's control and interference and their plans for me. I have written it all down, how it will be done. My plan is nothing like that of the whitecoats or the self-help anorexia books. There are things I can eat, and if I can just eat a bit more of them, then maybe this will keep them quiet and stop the questions about why I can't eat chocolate and cheese and so on. I'll make a lovely proposal, which I know will impress the nice lady doctor. I will increase my daily intake by 100 calories in week one, and then next week I will up it by another 100 and so on. It is the only way to make them leave me alone, and to make sure that they don't make me join those other girls.

I know I will still have to come to the hospital and get weighed and have friendly-style chats, but I actually think nice lady doctor will be relieved that I am not taking up so much of her time. She will be able to cross me off her 'danger' list and she can run off with her files and find someone else to feed.

I will keep moving on with my own plans. Staying still gives me the worst feelings – I get tired and lethargic and I feel so disgusted with myself, all agitated and bored in the crowded house. No, her methods will not work. Instead I will make a New Year's Resolution to get better and to succeed. I have never really failed; I don't like failures. It is best I don't allow this to become my first one. I will stay away from the scales – that will my most impressive feat, almost unbelievable. I will get to Cambridge. I will reinvent myself. I will say to myself:

'I have to get stronger to get better.'

'I miss my friends. I miss going out.'

'Life is slipping away from me every day. I just want my life back.'

This will motivate me to get better. And so I will. I will say it over and over again so that I can succeed. In the meantime I will continue to hide. I will continue to cover up my disgusting arms, and my bony face, and drape myself in baggy clothes so no one can see the outlines, so that I can blend into the background. So I can stop people staring. It is very hard to feel, when you can't find the edges of yourself.

Fourteen

'Surprise!'

'Happy New Me.'

I have taken it into my own hands. I am good at this. I have
made my own plan and it is something I can achieve. Everyone will be so surprised and pleased with me.

'Ten points for making this work for you,' they will tell
me.

'You can go back to being a normal girl now.'

And I will say, 'You see, you just have to do it on your
own. A few more calories every week for as long as it takes.
That's the way for me.'

They will marvel at how I can do it. But they forget my
willpower, remember? I sit in my bedroom and I draw up
my strategy. There are foods that I can eat – things from the
'Yes' list, and so I will just eat bigger quantities of them.
Instead of one tomato, I make it two, and instead of 100
grams of cottage cheese, I scribble down '150 grams'.

I come in from the pub and I go straight into the kitchen.

'Hello, I'm back.'

I take a plate (medium size) out of the cupboard (bang,
bang). Listen to me, in the kitchen. Listen to me eating. I
put small portions of my foods on to the plate: a piece of
processed ham, two crackers, half a carrot and three low-fat
crisps. The plate is full with a mix of different, brightly
coloured foods. I take it into the room where Mum and
Dad are sitting. I sit on the sofa and eat it all without stopping (chomp, chomp) and they watch me and I smile back

at them, and I put the plate down on the arm of the sofa and tuck my feet under my legs. See what I can do!

In my 400-calorie-a-day-week I have plenty of low-calorie bread. Sometimes the supermarket runs out, and I wonder if all the other anorexics have got there before me. I dip it in my reduced calorie Cup-a-Soup: a whole meal in under seventy calories. When I finish I need to clean it up. It's just the way I do things, or I start thinking about more food and it spirals. I could eat all day, I think, if I allowed myself. I don't allow myself, of course. I keep things bare and hollow and cold. I make sure that things are all placed and neat and ordered.

400, 500, 600, 700, 800 calories. . . Nearly at four figures . . . and counting.

My friends are back from university and I go to the pub with them to show them that I am are better. Can they see the difference? I can feel it. I can feel every sour mouthful for hours afterwards. They drink half-pints of lager and lime and I stick to my usual. Sometimes my Coke tastes like it might be the full-fat variety. I make sure I ask the barman more loudly next time, 'DIET Coke, my friend!'

If it is full-fat Coke, then things are out of place. I can't concentrate on the conversation because I am thinking of all the extra glucose and sugar and calories that will be turning to fat in my tummy. If that is the case, the 800-calorie-a-day plan is all out of sync and I don't know how to handle that, not yet.

My friends and some other girls talk about 'feeling fat'. I don't understand why they do that. I wonder if they are angry with me as well. I think they want to tell me that they deserve as much attention as me. Maybe they are just talking about what they want to talk about, things that they would say if I wasn't here. The loud girl with heavy black eyeliner, fake eyelashes and tousled hair talks about how she puts her fingers down her throat and makes herself sick. Someone else joins in, and they laugh at their greediness:

Girl 1: 'A whole packet of biscuits, a box of chocolates! It seems perfectly normal to retch it up into the toilet.'

Girl 2: 'I mean that much eating is just going too far, and it's only once in a while. It's the same as drinking too much, and making yourself sick so that you can drink more.'

They tell each other that they haven't eaten all day, just to get especially drunk. I start counting my six small food sessions. I curl up and try and block them out, but I keep catching bits of the food conversation, and I can't stop the counting.

That's eighty-five calories per biscuit and 4.5 grams of fat and so if she has a whole packet then that's 2,125 calories and even if she throws up she probably won't get it all out. Anyway, now she's drinking lager and lime and she doesn't know that it is over 100 calories and if she has five of those she has drunk near to what I have eaten all day. I'm sure she doesn't do this every day or she would be fatter. I have been looking at her arms and I think they might have got bigger. I need to look in more detail but I think she might have even put on weight. Maybe.

I sit on the loo in the pub. I bite my lip really hard until it bleeds, and a few tears make their way out of my eyes, but I am too cold to really cry. That is lucky because I don't want them to know I am like this. I know that they are trying to tell me something, even if they don't mean it, about how they are fed up with me having all the attention and hogging the limelight. I know this must be the reality of life; girls will talk about diets and their bodies. I just have to accept it. I suppose I have to be strong. It is not their fault; it is mine.

They will be glad to know that I am forcing in the fats gram by gram without looking, so I can start to get away from all of them. Run away. Run right away.

Fifteen

When I booked the holiday to Rhodes with my friend I didn't forget that there would be no diet bread and diet soup in Greece, I just thought more about escaping. I thought about being able to smoke my cigarettes in public places without choking on my fast-pumping heart. Usually I am scared of being spotted by my mum and dad doing a bad thing like smoking. Every night I have a cigarette out of my bedroom window. I sit on the edge of the windowsill, blowing the smoke as far away from the house as possible, fanning it away with my hands, then I dart back into bed, diving deep under the duvet with the imagined sound of footsteps, my cigarette tossed wildly into the freezing black air.

But on holiday I can smoke freely, which sounds a funny reason to go on holiday, but that is my reason. I can also get a tan, which might mean that I will dare to expose my thin arms in public. My best friend is coming with me. She is kind because she hasn't asked me about what I will eat in another country, and what she will do if she gets hungry and wants a packet of crisps or something, like normal people do. I use some of the money that my family has put aside for me for university, which I keep spending. I don't mean to keep wasting it on non-achievement-related items. I feel guilty for it; I am not at university because of my let-down. I must have let everybody down.

My dad drives my friend and me to the airport. I know he thinks it is strange that he is taking his faded, eldest, childlike, breakable-bones daughter to the airport to go on a package holiday in the sun. I know that because I can see it in his face, even though he doesn't say much, because he can't, because I have hurt the family and because it is all too much for him. He has got angry with me a couple of times because I wanted to drive the car (which I can do, because I passed my test) but he says that I don't have the strength and that I am a 'danger to the roads'. I prefer it when he is quiet; that is easier for me. I know he thinks that going on holiday will make me worse. I don't think anyone is happy about it, because they still think that I don't really have enough energy to walk to town, let alone go on an 18–30s package holiday, but things are changing, can't they see that?

When I get to the airport departure lounge I can't believe it when I order a bottle of alcoholic lemonade. I just walk up to the bar and I order it. When I drink it I feel dizzy-high, and I want another one, but then we have to get on the plane and I am counting the extra calories all the way there. I feel as though I should be happy because I just did something really good, but I don't feel happy or sad at the moment, just controlled and uncontrolled. These are a much more scary set of opposites, because uncontrollable equals unbearable.

We get to the hotel late and usually I am not up late, so the whole thing disorientates me and I can't sleep. I don't sleep at the moment; I am super-alert. It is a strange feeling. I look at the clock and it is three in the morning. I have been lying under the cold, white sheets in the white-tiled room. I have been drifting in a banging kind of a daze. My body jumps and moves and it feels like I am on the top level of sleep, next to awake. I am thinking about what I am going to eat for breakfast and how I must sunbathe for at least six hours a day and swim for one hour a day, so as not to let things get out of order.

There is no kitchen here and no skimmed milk, and no

scales to weigh out my portions. We go to the bar for breakfast, but because we are late we have missed it, so my friend orders an orange juice and I order a Coke. I daren't ask for a Diet Coke in case they don't understand, or in case they look at me strangely, which I wouldn't like.

It is easy to get drunk here. There are bars full of cocktails and happy hours and the alcoholic lemonade is still jumping on my tongue. It makes it easier if you are drunk to deal with the bread, chips, fried things and kebabs. I would never touch these kinds of foods at home but for some inexplicable reason I can here. It doesn't feel real, it is like I am sleepwalking through every day. We go out, my friend and I, on an organized bar crawl. In one of the pubs we have to stand in a line and down shots of strange spirits one by one and play party games. In the darkness/drunkenness, I manage to throw my drink over my shoulder on to the floor behind me. I can't drink it when I am forced like that. As people come close to me, I start to panic.

Don't make me. Don't make me. Get out, get out.

The music is loud and it hurts my head. The people are too noisy and too close to my skin.

It is hard when you are lying by the pool and there are hours until dinnertime. Other people are reading books and listening to Walkmans and falling asleep. I am sitting up, lying down, jumping in the pool, walking up to the room, sighing, coming back to the pool, getting hot and feeling like I need to put something in my mouth to stop the overthinking. I walk to the shop and buy some fruit sweets. I eat the whole packet by the pool, frantically chewing, and then smoke one cigarette after another and pretend to rest. Nothing rests in me – everything moves and flips and jumps and spins and does cartwheels and then dives and lurches.

When I speak to my friend, I cry, but only once, because now I have force-fed myself a bit everything must be better.

I have a tan and I am a bit fatter. I must definitely be fatter, and so they will all be pleased with me.

After the eating and drinking holiday (I am not sure how I just did that), I feel like I must be a lot bigger. With every forkful I felt myself grow and widen. I get home to Mum and Dad but they don't seem to think that I have been transformed. I have been eating to make them feel better because they were feeling sad about things, but it doesn't seem to have any immediate effect. I am sure the whitecoats have told them to think that I am always deceiving them, which is not necessarily my intention.

I ask my dad for a lift to town to see my friends, and to half-listen to their conversations. I walk into the pub and people seem happy to see me. I think they are shocked when I order a Bacardi Breezer. They are all staring at me.

It's just a drink, or two, or three. Yes, I have got fatter, thanks for commenting on how well I look.

I block my ears and float around. I am not going backwards. I am going forwards, and so that means lots of drinking, dancing and forgetting things because they are all too strange and blurry to cope with.

I am glad that they let me work in the pub now. I spend most of my time there, eating thick, salty, full-flavoured crisps and drinking alcopops and going out with students who are mad and drunk and fun-out-of-control. I serve the hungry customers with hot food from under the hot plate. I am shaking with the weight of the plates piled high with beef and potatoes and Yorkshire puddings and vegetables and gravy. I am walking through the hot, smelly pub and my arms are straining as I carry the steaming plates to the beer-filled tables, in my thick black woollen tights under my thick black trousers. I like feeding people. At the end of the lunchtime rush, I get to sit down and eat my food with the rest of the staff. They get excited about the free Sunday lunch and pile their plates high, talking about the rich lamb and thick gravy. I take a big plate of salad with tablespoons of pickle. I like the taste of the pickle – a strong taste on my tongue. This is against the rules, because salad is not part of the staff meal deal at the pub, but no one dares tell me because they are so pleased that I am eating something. I can see them, though; they just can't help looking at my green and brown plate.

I asked my GP to write a letter saying that going to work would be good for my health. I convinced him that I needed something to do to make me socialize and feel a part of teenage life, instead of sitting in front of the TV on my own all day. He didn't seem to know that much about eating disorders. He seemed a bit embarrassed so I was too. He has been my GP ever since I was a little girl when I had chicken pox and measles and running noses; normal illnesses he could solve with antibiotics and sugary medicine. I don't think he quite understands why I can't eat. I must be strange if even he thinks that. I thought he would understand all medical things but, for some reason, I think this one is different. I think it is because I am a girl and he thinks that this is an illness that little girls get, and he is not a girl, and he doesn't seem to understand it simply because of that.

Sixteen

Pretty girls, I see them everywhere. Ones that other people may have missed because they only cross the eye for a second, but I take them all in. Things like that don't blend in for me. I see it all. Everything pricks me hard. There are girls sipping white wine, with beery boyfriends on their arms, and they have perfect seamless figures. I watch their thighs, and there is no dimpling or wobbling, their legs seem to be welded apart, they don't rub together as they walk. They are all taller and thinner than me. I watch them on the streets, in the pub, the shops, the magazines, and I wonder if they were born that way. Are they natural or are they shutting themselves up in the bathroom and flushing their insides down the toilet? Maybe they are all at it in secret, and are trying to get me to stop so that they can win and be better and slimmer and neat-edged. This is what I am thinking every time I have to eat more. It makes it hard, but I am trying to get back to normality.

People look at me with different eyes now that I am a bit bigger, a bit more normal-shaped. Suddenly, they almost see me as I was before, even though I am no longer the same. I have small curves, which I can just about grab in my hands and squash – I spent a long time trying to get rid of this. Strangers have stopped staring in the same way. I am almost acceptable now that I am sevenish stone. People are not sure of their reactions. They look at each other, and then at me, and then they squint their eyes as if they are trying to figure me out. So I keep quiet. I merge into the background. I take deep breaths before I feel sure enough to speak. I want to submerge, hold back and listen like a little body should.

When people bring up the subject of doctors and weight I do my 'What are you making a fuss about?' incredulous look. I flash some of my dinner in their face. They keep on testing me, of course, but I won't relent. I keep munching right through the fatty-soaked Chinese food they put in front of me, and the thick and spicy Indian curry and I smile wide and drink another orange Bacardi Breezer. I have abandoned the calorie-counting in public. I reserve this for my private moments – the in-between parts (of which there are many). I fluctuate between control and crazy eating (well, crazy for me, anyway).

Lovely Mum and Dad sit on the sofa and watch me. I know what they are thinking. I am sure of it. They are wondering what they could possibly have done wrong to end up with me in this state. I know that they probably don't trust me. I know that they think that my food is not normal food. I know their secret conversations. I have a good imagination, a really scary one too.

'She's definitely eating more – isn't she?'

'That must be a good thing – mustn't it?'

'It might even mean that she's better – right?'

'Does this mean we don't have to go to the eating disorders support group one evening a week after a tiring day at work, and listen to more stories of starving, cottage-cheese-eating teenagers?'

'Please tell me this is true.'

'I don't know.'

New people that I meet don't even know about my eating problems, I think. They treat me like I am completely normal. They think I am shy and curled up, and that I am naturally quiet. I let them think that. I let them think that is me. I don't wear any bandages so they can't tell what is in my head. Men start to come closer to me now, like it is acceptable, because I have these little curves. I want them to like me. I want them to desire me. But they won't like me if I get any bigger. I need to stay small.

In the dark, in the club, I sometimes tell them more than I should. Words spurt from my mouth and I am telling strangers about this little illness I had a few weeks ago, and the feelings I had.

To Boy 1: 'Hello. We get on but you don't know me. You can't really know me until I tell you this thing about me. I used to be anorexic. That means I got very thin – I was five and a bit stone. You seem shocked. Yes, I look OK now. I'm fine now. I decided to get over it. I work in the pub. Things are better; really they are fine. It's just it is such a big part of me that I don't want to be your girlfriend unless you understand this. I know we only met this evening, but when I'm drunk I become really honest about things. I prefer it to be that way. Sure, I'll come outside with you. I'm so flattered that you think I'm gorgeous. No one says that to me any more. I feel really drunk. Let's go and talk outside. Oh, you kissed me. This is what I should be doing, like a normal teenage girl. Thanks for your number, but I won't be speaking to you again, or telling anyone about this. God, I shouldn't have shared all this with you. I can hardly see your face. I can't even remember your name.'

To Boy 2: 'Thanks for the cheese sandwich. How did I get to your house? I think my friend likes your friend. They're laughing in the other room. Oh, you're kissing me. Look, there is something you need to know about me. Thanks for understanding and holding me so tightly. You aren't really my type. You're a personal trainer? You could do a diet plan and exercise plan for me. I think everything would be all right if I had a professional exercise plan, then I could get the muscled, tight legs that I want. Don't you think? You look like you could take care of me. It is a shame I can't call you again. Cheese sandwiches at three in the morning aren't something I should repeat. It upsets my routine.'

To Boy 3: 'You thought I looked horrible before. I saw you looking at me and wondering how I could have changed so much, so quickly. Thanks for at least pretending you still liked me then with your letters and your phone calls (on and off) depending on how much you could cope with my strangely subdued voice at the end of the phone. I know you didn't like me, not when I looked like that – who would? When we met I was on the edge of a new life, going to university, and it was all fun. Do you remember kissing me after the office trip to the pub? I was on work experience and I fancied you, and you liked me back. And then the next week you were landed with a new me. It was kind of you to keep in touch, when I was a very different person from the one you thought. Now it's obvious you like me. Boys seem to like girls who are size eight, even if they say that they don't. You can't believe your luck. You tell me you have fallen for me. It sounds so romantic, I think. I don't feel anything like that, but I accept the nice compliment. Did you see my ex-boyfriend in the pub with his pretty, curvy girlfriend? It makes me sad to look at him. There are silences in our conversation. I can't think of anything to say to you that you might be interested in, or that I might be interested in – sorry.'

I see my ex-boyfriend. He is driving a blue Fiesta and his new girlfriend sits in the passenger seat. He doesn't see me because he isn't looking for me, because I am out of his life and she is in it, but I see him. I see him everywhere, even when he is not there. I catch glimpses of his face on the edge of others. I write about him every day in my diary because I miss him, or maybe I just miss us, and the old me, eating spaghetti at his house and ordinary things I used to do. He looks guilty when he does see me, because he thinks that he let me down. He thinks that he should have helped me more, I know, he told me. But I tell him not to worry because, 'I'm fine. I'm all better. I'm seeing other people now, so the old story of us is closed. I'm not going to go to the doctor any more, everything is all better. How is *she*, by the way?'

After I see him I feel a bit shaky. I walk up to my old school to meet my little sisters. I don't look up in case anyone sees me, and they have heard about my messed-up head. I don't want to speak to anyone in case they know that I didn't go to university, and that I am one of 'those girls' (which they surely do, because everyone knows everything here). My teacher sees me and smiles. He makes me talk. I don't want to talk. I want to walk past him so that he doesn't have to think about me. If he hadn't seen me, he wouldn't have had to think about me. He would have just forgotten about me and got on with his day. Instead, he has to make some small talk and look concerned. He says the wrong thing. People always say the wrong thing. He says, 'You look well.'

He must not have met a real anorexic before.

Well! Well! Fat. Fat — that is what he means. You look well — plump, round, healthy therefore fat, definitely fatter than the last time he saw you.

I wish I hadn't gone out. I wish I could make them all forget. I don't think they are ever going to forget, are they? They are always going to remember me this way. I have fought away my fear to make them all happy, and they still look at me in that strange way and try to make nice and caring conversation. For those who know me it may always be this way.

I am moulding myself to fit into the ideal shapes that the doctors and the strangers and the family and society prescribe for me. Then they will let me go away and I can make things the way I want them to. For the moment, I need to curve myself more, so I will. They are all measuring me and sizing me up, so it all has to be as convincing as possible. The nice lady doctor seems to think that if I get to the 'ideal weight' my mind will flip over to her side, that I will somehow gain this understanding again. So I push my mind away. I sit in my bath of spiders every day and let them crawl over me. I wrap the snakes round my neck. I stand at the edge of the top of the highest building and let you push me. I don't fall. I won't fall.

'You have been so brave – you really have done so well. Do you think you would like to continue to see me? I'm here if you need me. When you come back from university you should make sure you check in every holiday, so we can monitor your progress.' Nice lady doctor smiles.

'That would be delightful. Thank you so much,' I say.

I glide into the weighing room and nod at the rising scales.

'Well done, you! You have put on two pounds,' she informs me.

'Yes, it seems that I have put on two pounds.' I smile back as I say this because it is supposed to be a very good thing.

Thank you, dear lady doctor, I am thrilled. I am truly delirious to have made you happy, and what a great job you have done! Although, surely, you know that I will never be coming back here. I will not be speaking to your busy receptionists any more, ever. I am fine now. There is no need for you, and your scales, and your thirty-minute chats, and my superficial smile as I wait for hours on end to see you. Actually, I need to go. I have bought a new dress, which is a size ten. It hangs off my shoulders, it slips off my arms and you can see my new padded bra underneath. I am going out drinking with my friends. My favourite cocktail is one full of cream. I bet you are very pleased with that. Goodbye, nice lady doctor. You should go, as I am sure there is another emergency right round the corner. You really are so much nicer than Dr Whitecoat. He said that I didn't have a chance of getting away, and look, I have.

Please don't blame yourself. I am an excellent actress. Sometimes, you know, I sit in bed and I can't believe I actually managed to get up and force myself through the day with such confidence. I can spend the whole day lying. I don't actually tell any lies, I just act out one big one. I feel guilty for that. I don't want to let you down. I would really like to fold up within myself. Things might be better like that. I should be able to get properly depressed, but I can't. Sometimes I can't even make myself cry. Even if I think of the saddest part of me there is just a blankness. I don't have much to say, so I stare in the mirror until I lose myself. I have lost myself. I have lost what I was. I try and force myself to feel and when I manage to prick up the tears, I watch my reflection in the mirror, tears rolling down my face. I try and see if I can work out what they are doing. I step outside myself.

What am I? What am I, now?

Turnaround

The order of my story now appears to be: child, teenager, anorexic, then not-an-anorexic. As quickly as I was labelled an anorexic, I was no longer one, not an official one, anyway. One day I made a decision to turn things round; it was New Year and so I thought I should make a resolution. My resolution was to end my eating disorder. Just like that. At five and a half stone I simply changed my mind.

I would have expected the story (had it not been my own) to have a more forceful twist. I would have expected somebody to get a proper grip on me and shake things out of my control. Surely, anorexics are put into special centres where a diet is constructed for them, where it is ensured they gain weight week on week and where they are watched and monitored with close scrutiny? This is the case for some, but not for others. Anorexics are often difficult and stubborn to treat; it is not an easy task. Because of this, there is a range of very different treatments suited to the individuals involved, there isn't a one-size-fits-all approach. Often there is a multi-disciplinary approach, with a whole team of professionals dealing with various aspects of the anorexic's behaviour, both the causes and the symptoms. This level of intervention may be more the case at the life-threatening end of the scale, but as my weight was not evaluated to be that, this experience was not the reality for me, or for many others. There simply don't seem to be the resources for those on the cliff edge of severity. I just wasn't a priority unless I made myself into one. Ironically, I needed to carry on self-destructing in order for me to get more treatment, and for some reason I decided not to do that.

My initial sit-up-and-do-something change was actually filled with the needs of others. I could no longer deal with everyone else's depression and anger. I could no longer take the transparent stares and the sharp look-aways of the shoppers in Sainsbury's. In reality, I had no desire to be anything in particular, not well, ill or anorexic; I retained only a reflex response to make other people happy. I needed (wrongly or rightly) to resurrect some part of the good girl for other people. I was embarrassed that I had created a version of myself which was the opposite of the achieving and successful me. I made up stories about how I was feeling to reassure other people, rather than actually experiencing that set of emotions for myself. There were stories about how 'great' it felt to be an acceptable weight and how 'great' it was to be able to fit into clothes from the shops. There were stories about how 'fun!' it was to get so drunk that I couldn't stand up. Then there were stories about how I was 'feeling so much better'. These were the things that other people wanted to hear. Everyone around me was cautiously willing to accept my change, because it was the relief that was so longed for and so needed. It was much easier to think that I was fixed. That is, after all, what everyone had been hoping for, for months. As I ate more, and refigured myself ten months after diagnosis, I removed my anorexic label, I dispatched the psychiatrists, I rationalized and objectified my problems and there was a sigh of relief all round.

Anorexics often do depersonalize their actions in this way, as if what is happening to them is an entirely passive experience. They manage to sustain a sense of distance from their body; they tiptoe round the edge of feeling. They can't be a part of what they are doing because to admit it would mean collapse. So they just look on.

I remember thinking to myself, 'I must now be on the verge of fainting.'

But I didn't feel weak or light-headed. I watched myself fall over on the carpet, and then I got up and went to watch TV, and I didn't tell anybody and nobody saw me, so it didn't happen. It was simple like that. I just framed myself in different states.

During my decline, I liked to read about all of the theories on the causes of anorexia, and say to myself, 'Hmmmm, perhaps these things are happening to me. How interesting.' Then I would get out my pen and underline the relevant bits in the book, and I would write quotes down in my note-book and think, 'This is really important.' But I would not know why, and I would not think of it as me, or me as it. The objectification of myself was a survival instinct – it was the only way to survive the self-destruction.

By responding only to the illusion of myself, I was as equally capable of removing myself from the self-starving as I was able to fall into it. I looked over the object of me, and made the decision that things needed to change. Could it have been the willpower that so neatly edged me into my anorexia that was the answer to me getting out of it? It is difficult to explain why this decision couldn't have been made before. It is frustrating to think that this could have potentially come from within me all along, but I don't think that is the case. The issue needed to be brought out by other people for me to recognize the seriousness of it. I had to get to a stage where I felt so helpless and weakened to real-ize that the control that I thought I had was not actually there at all.

But the story does not end because I decided to put my finger over my lip and said 'shhhhhhhh' or because I moved the setting of the scene. If anorexia is really defined only by weight – a few pounds here or there – then this would be the beginning of the end of my story and I could stop my secret here. In fact, what can occur is that emotions, feelings and secrets go further in, and become even more closed-up. In the first part of anorexia things are body-side – it is hard to stop the outside world knowing because they can see for themselves. After weight is put on, things go inside, well away from public view.

PART 4

Stories of Grace

Seventeen

'Hi, I'm Grace. It's nice to meet you.'

Grace smiles at the girl who is showing her to her university room. Mum and Dad stand at her side. The girl smiles back. She seems friendly, Grace thinks. She is also very small and slim. She looks Grace up and down, registering the new arrival, checking out the competition. Grace weighs seven stone and six pounds. The doctors have said that this is still below the ideal Body Mass Index for her height, but Grace disagrees. Grace has decided that she does not want to lose any weight, but neither does she want to put any on. Gaining weight would not be an easy thing to deal with, and therefore it is best to just keep an equilibrium, which will keep everyone around her happy(ish). This is all she can allow them to be.

The thin, pretty girl smiles at Grace as she leaves. 'We have a girls' football team. I'm the captain, if you want to try out?'

'Thank you, yes, that sounds great,' Grace responds politely.

Grace does not know if she likes football, or if she likes other girls, or if she likes team sports, or if she would be brave enough to try something that she might not be very good at, but she wants the thin, pretty girl to like her and so she says yes.

Mum and Dad decide to leave. Grace watches them out of her bedroom window, which overlooks the river. They stand on the pathway and wave at her. Tears well up.

Mummy, Daddy, don't go. Don't leave me. I can't do it. Maybe I can't, after all.

Grace waves back and watches them, hand-holding, gripping each other – tightly. Grace thinks of the cigarettes that she can smoke and the exercises she can do in the privacy of her own room, with no one watching her or making judgements and passing comment.

Grace decides that the best thing to do is to try and find someone to talk to and make friends with. She walks up and down the corridors banging the big, heavy doors behind her. She walks round in circles. Everything is silent. She is probably early. She is always early, always over-prepared, always ahead of time. She goes back to the room. She stands in the echoing silence and decides to unpack some cases. There is a big box of food. Grace went to Sainsbury's with Dad to pick out all of her favourite things – her usual foods so that she doesn't have to eat the college food if it is not on her accepted list.

Grace unpacks most of her cases. She makes the room nice and tidy, all the boxes are put away. The room is much bigger than her bedroom at home and so it feels empty, with most of her things packed into the huge cupboards. Everything is so much bigger than she had imagined it would be.

Grace sits in another student's room. There are special introductory meetings with people from the year above to make the new students feel comfortable. The two boys in charge hand around mugs of tea and chocolate digestives. Grace's eyes widen as the plate makes its way around. Grace doesn't eat biscuits. Everybody takes one (even the girls!). Grace quickly grabs a biscuit from the plate, just so that she doesn't stand out. This is not what she had intended, her sort-of-a-plan to keep things in balance is not going to be easy. Some of the boys and girls drink bottles of beer. Grace sips her tea and thinks of a way to excuse herself.

First-year Freshers also get a first-night welcome dinner, a formal occasion where everyone has to wear special black gowns. On the menu is a three-course meal including chocolate pudding, port, coffee and further chocolates. Grace swallows it all down to make sure that no one thinks that the thin girl has a problem. It is the strangest day, everything is out of place, off centre. It gives her a thumping head that night thinking about all the thousands of calories she has eaten just to fit in. She can't sleep because she is busy trying to calculate the numbers, but it is impossible because she has never eaten some of those foods before, and she does not know their value.

200 for bread and approximately 600 for the pudding and the chocolates and then there was some orange juice I drank earlier, plus breakfast and lunch . . . and the wine.

The numbers end up so big that she loses count.

First morning in college and things are out of focus. Grace is up early before the alarm, pacing the room and wondering when to go to the breakfast hall. A girl from along the corridor knocks on the door.

'Hi, Gracie, you coming to breakfast?'

'Yeh, sure, great.'

Please like me. I'll do whatever you want to do.

In the breakfast hall there are people nervously chatting. Grace hopes that they won't notice that she is having a different breakfast from the rest of them. She manages some cereal.

Stop looking at me. I don't eat fry-ups. They are disgusting. What is so strange about me? I ate the whole dinner last night, isn't that good enough for you? I proved it, OK? There are just some things that I don't eat, even though I am all better now. I don't eat: chips, crisps, pizza, cheese, ice cream, any fast food, any fried food, pastries, butter, chocolate, sweets, puddings, red meat,

*Coke (unless Diet). I will never touch them, not unless I am out
of control. I am just eating healthily. OK?*

Grace shuffles in the plastic seat. She can't wait to leave
the table and go back to her room to sit on her own and
smoke a cigarette. She decides that this will be the last time,
definitely, that she breaks her rules. People will just have to
get used to it. She will mend it tomorrow, she will get things
back on track. Not in a backwards way, though. She is
certainly not ill any more, no way. No help required here.

It is 6.30 a.m. Grace is awake. The noise is too loud to stay
in bed – the noise in her head from her own inside voice,
played on the wrong speed, the wrong RPM. It still hits her
as soon as she wakes up. The rest of the college is silent.
She senses the sleeping hung-over bodies in the rooms next
to hers.

Get out, out, out.

She jumps out of bed and puts on her tracksuit and
running shoes. She doesn't open the curtains; it is dark
outside. She creeps out of her room, as silently as she can,
shuffles down the steps and runs towards the back gate of
the college. It is a cold, frosted morning. Her breath hangs
on the air in front of her. She keeps her head down and
her footsteps light, as she skips her way out of the college
grounds.

Don't hear me. Don't see me. I'm not really here.

She takes a big, huge, freeing breath. She loves her morning runs, not the running part (she hates that. It hurts. She
struggles. She has never been a good runner, she has never
had much physical strength) but the feeling at the end of it.

I've escaped. I am out.

She does not have the energy to go far, or fast, but as
long as she keeps moving and pounding her feet on the
gravel then things are OK. Things are in balance. She jogs

along the back alley behind the college, across the road and she runs by the foggy river, then back along the main street. She keeps her head down under her hat so that no one spots her.

Don't spot me. Don't think I'm strange, I'm not different. I'm fine. Perfectly normal to be running.

She sneaks back into college and dashes to the bathroom to stand under a hot shower. No one has seen her. No one has woken up yet, and she is already ahead. She pulls on her clothes straight away, before she is dry, so that she cannot see or feel her body. She holds in her stomach.

Yuk, fat, yuk.

Grace moves around the room, tidying and moving pieces of paper from one side of the desk to the other. She keeps going, keeps moving. She doesn't like to sit with herself. She is wet and cosy in her warm clothes. She needs to have something to eat, to stop her thinking about food any longer. She has bags of muesli (diet and sugar-free) stored in her special food cupboard. She pours herself a big bowl and covers it in skimmed milk. She sits in the armchair in the corner of the room and watches every mouthful from the bowl to the spoon and into her mouth. When she has finished, she pours some more. Never a full bowl, but half a bowl, to stop the ringing voices.

The only person who sees her eating is the cleaning lady who comes into the room to collect the wastepaper bin.

''Morning, love. You OK today?'

'Great. Fine. Thanks.'

Grace isn't one for chatter when she is eating. She wonders what the cleaning lady thinks about her, when every day, at an early hour, she is sitting in her chair all alone, eating her diet muesli. Grace imagines the dissenting voices of the whitecoats who would tell her that, 'This is not normal behaviour. You could try eating with other people in college.

What about just trying to eat a fry-up with bacon and sausages? Try and let go of your control. Why not just eat a little bit of fried bread?'

Fat fat fat dripping off everything. No way. It's fine not to eat those things. Leave me alone.

Grace walks quickly to her lectures. She is always early and always turns up, unlike most people who don't go to lectures because they aren't compulsory. The other students on the course think that Grace is very controlled. They always say:

'Grace will have done her essay on time.'

'Grace is thin and toned.'

'Grace will know where we are supposed to go.'

'Grace eats nice and healthy.'

Grace thinks they are right, but she wishes that they wouldn't make a point of it. She has to work hard to get to the top again, and things are much more difficult here than they were at school. Everyone seems to be loud and clever and talkative. A lot of people spent time at schools where getting into Oxbridge was their only goal. They are very clever. Grace wonders if she really deserves to be here. She has to lock herself away at her desk and push really hard, late nights, early mornings. Better, much better, best.

Grace turns twenty in her second week at Cambridge. It is a year on from the cold, crying nineteenth birthday. A year on from people leaving, Boyfriend leaving, weight drop, drop, dropping off. Most of the people in Grace's year are only eighteen or nineteen. Many of them have been travelling and have done some amazing things in Third World countries. Grace can't imagine what that must be like, to be away in another country, on your own; she can't even see an image in her head. Some of the other students have come straight from school. All they can talk about is their A-level results, their school uniforms and their teachers. Nothing really fits with Grace's story. No one has a story like hers, or at least not one that they are willing to share. Grace has to make up some stories to be normal and to explain things.

Story number one:
'Hello. My name is Grace. I took a year off because I had glandular fever. I got it the week before I was supposed to go to university, can you believe it? I had my suitcases packed and I had bought pots and pans as well. I was really ill and so they said I shouldn't do something as stressful as start university. I had a place somewhere else actually, but then I decided to rethink, so I am here now. I thought I should make the best of a bad situation. It took a few months to really recover and sometimes I feel weak because of the repercussions. I get ill sometimes because of it, it sort of hangs around. I am fine now, though.'

Story number two:
'Hello. My name is Grace. I come from the north-east of England (no, that is not Manchester). I'm studying English. It feels really strange, doesn't it, to actually be here. Does it look like you thought it would? I imagined it differently. I kept reimagining it, making it look different ways inside. But we made it here, didn't we? Are you like me? Are we the same, or similar? I am very friendly, just like you. I worked in a pub in my year off, just to get some money together and to have a break. I liked working behind a bar. I wanted to do something 'real', you know, explore what that was like, away from the studying and from the pressure. It's great fun to be here, isn't it?'

Story number three: (reserved for best friends or very drunken conversations) 'Hello. My name is Grace. I know you a bit better now and I think we might be proper friends. But you can't really know me unless I tell you about why I really had a year off. I had a problem with food and the doctors said that I was anorexic. That's why I have got so many different sizes of clothes in my wardrobe. Some of ·them don't fit any more. Anyway, I'm fine now, but that's why I might be a bit quiet sometimes. It was only a small problem. I got over it very quickly. It never got that bad, not to a hospitalization level, anyway. I worked it out all on my own. Nobody really helped me much, but I think it is better that way. Anyway, let's not talk about it. Let's go out and have some fun. It's all over now and I'm a normal student. Over. Finished.'

Grace worries that she has let the true story slip through too many times. She told her new best friends and they seemed to be very understanding. They both went to boarding school and said there were lots of people there who had anorexia and bulimia. Grace's school was different from theirs, *so* different – at her school there were more pregnant sixteen-year-old girls than skinny intellectual ones – it wasn't cool to be that way.

Grace tells a few other people the real story. She doesn't mean to. It is dark and drunken in the college bar and she doesn't really know what to say. It fills awkward silences with strange people. At least it is an interesting story, rather than the other ones about where she comes from, and her northern state school, which seem to be boring in comparison to everyone else's. Anyway, there is not much else she can say about herself. Anorexia has been her life and the things before it seem somewhat irrelevant now.

She wakes up the day after the night in the college bar and shouts at herself. She decides that it is best to just avoid those people, and hopes that they were too drunk to remember, anyway. It is now possible, however, that everyone knows, and that they will see her altogether differently.

Stupid girl. I wasn't meant to let it out. Not to anyone. It was going to be a new me.

Grace decides that she shouldn't talk to anyone in much detail again, but the story seems to drip out of her, like she can't contain it. She is still overflowing with it.

Stop it up.

Story number four:

'I used to have a boyfriend. We were together for two years and I loved him. We were a perfect couple, but then he went off with someone else. No, no, I'm not sure why. We were just very different. I was desperate to get away from the place where we grew up and he wanted to stay there. I just feel like being single now. It's more fun. I think a boyfriend might get in the way.

'I am sort of seeing this boy at college, but it has to be a secret. We were in the bar and I was dancing on a chair, and I stared at him until he noticed me. I can do that – I can get a reaction if I try hard enough. But he isn't my boyfriend because he has a girlfriend at home, and she's a model. I don't know why I picked a boy like that to get obsessed with, but I did. Now I keep staring at him all the time. I have seen the pictures of his model girlfriend who is very thin and pretty, but I think that means that I need to be thin and pretty because he wants to see me, too. I keep thinking about the size and shape of my growing thighs and how I must make sure they look the best, so that he will still like me. I really want him to like me, because that makes me feel nice . . . nicer.'

Grace's stories are mixed up. She can't remember which bits she has told to which person and which act she has to put on for whom. It is better to keep a bit of a distance, she decides. It is best to start a new chapter and leave the old ones at the back of her memory – just let them slip away. It is easier to be friendly, it is easier to go to the college bar and join in with the drunken nights, and leave the old Grace behind and have a sort-of-fun time. It just takes a bit of time to learn how to answer people's questions. Sometimes it is better not to say anything, not to give too much away, but that is hard, when you feel like it needs to come out.

Grace likes the attention from the boys in college. It makes her forget herself. It gives her a nice feeling when they like her. Some people don't like this behaviour, though. The girls in the year above don't want her getting the attention. They write about her in the college gossip magazine. They call her a 'Dis-Grace' because they think she has been flirting with some boys in their year. The girls think that they are very funny, coining such an apt phrase. Clever Cambridge students. Grace doesn't think it is funny. She tries to imagine what Mum might say if she told her about their attacking words (which she wouldn't, because she wouldn't want Mum to think that she wasn't having a nice time): 'They're just jealous.'

But it doesn't seem to help. Grace sits in her room and cries. She is supposed to go for mince pies and wine at the College President's rooms.

Everyone will know. Everyone hates me. They are all laughing and bitching about me. Having secret whispers behind my back. I don't understand what I have done wrong. I don't know what I am supposed to say to make it better.

Grace decides not to go to the drinks party. She doesn't know how to react. She feels like shouting out: 'I have had anorexia, and people have been most worried that I will get even thinner and die, if they are too nasty to me.'

Over the last year or so people have been scared of Grace, and have not known what to say to her.

'Weirdo.'

'Thin-girl.'

'Freak.'

They weren't able to talk to her because it made them uncomfortable. They didn't understand what she was doing, and so they stayed away and kept quiet. Now it seems that everyone talks to her. They say what they like, and act exactly how they want to, because anorexia is no longer a shield. Grace decides to hide in her room. She decides that she will not be the sociable, drunken, college person that she thought she should be, because that route has not been successful. She will stay away, so they can't find out any more about her and they can't hurt her. She will just be a different Grace. A quiet Grace; a Grace that no one can write things about. She decides that this is a better strategy because it means that she won't have to go to so many parties and drink creamy cocktails and eat student meals. It will be better if she sits at her desk, and works hard at reading all the plays of Shakespeare, and tries to be the best, and eats her WeightWatchers' soup.

Eighteen

Grace smiles at her friend and says goodbye, hazy-drunk, at the door of her college room. She walks in and puts her coat on the bed. She sits down at the edge of the bed and hurriedly pulls off her shoes. She walks to the bathroom and shuts the door. She looks in the mirror and sighs. She washes her hands under the cold tap, flicking off the excess water. She takes her hands behind her head and pulls her hair back, twisting it away from her face. She takes the bobble from her wrist and ties the hair loosely up. She looks in the mirror again.

Right, Grace. This has to be done.

Grace walks towards the toilet. She leans over the toilet, facing the bowl, legs slightly bent. She places her hand at the edge of her mouth. She puts the first two fingers of her right hand into her mouth until she feels the back of her mouth, and then the throat, pushing down on her tongue and sliding and inching the fingers back. She repeats this a couple of times, removing them as she coughs, splutters and retches. After a few attempts of pushing the fingers down into the base of her throat, she jerks and pulls her fingers out, as the sick bursts out of her mouth. She then quickly sticks her fingers back down her throat, she coughs and more sick comes up. She takes a breath and wipes her mouth. She walks to the mirror and looks at her face.

Come on, Grace, just one more time. That will be enough. See how much better you feel already.

She walks back to the toilet, bends over, left hand on left thigh, right fingers in the mouth and throat. She repeats the action until there is coughing and retching and the sick isn't coming out with such force. She walks back to the mirror. There are tears running down her blotchy face. She takes her shaky and reddened, tooth-marked hand and picks up a glass by the sink. She fills it with cold water. She drinks, swirling the water around her mouth and her sore, aching throat and spits it into the sink before taking a gulp. She walks over to the toilet and grabs some toilet roll to wipe the seat, inside and out. Then she looks at the sick in the toilet as if to measure the volume capacity, and pulls the chain. Next she picks up some bleach and pours it down the toilet. Another flush and it is all gone. Then she sprays the room with air freshener. She leaves the bathroom and immediately returns, lifting up the toilet lid and checking under the rim, just to be safe. She then walks to the sink and looks in the mirror above it. She cries a few tears and watches them run down her face. She picks up her tooth-brush, puts a large blob of toothpaste on it and brushes her teeth. She washes her mouth out with sharp, burning, minty mouthwash and sighs.

There is a knock on the door. Grace takes a look around the bathroom, frantically checking for signs.

'I'm in the bathroom, I won't be a minute.'

She runs to the door with her freshly brushed teeth, smiles and welcomes her friends inside. Her heart is racing and pumping. She feels full of a delicious energy.

'Do you want something to drink?' Grace enquires.

They haven't got a clue, she thinks to herself. They have still got their dinner inside them. Grace chatters on, rapidly, full of energy, buzzing and pulsing with excitement. See how I do this, she thinks to herself – see how good I am at this! At last.

Grace turns the light off and gets into bed. She thinks about what she will eat in the morning. Because she has been sick, and has got rid of all the bad foods from the evening (the wine and the chocolate), she can have a really nice morning. Things are peaceful for once as she closes her eyes. She feels a bit bad for doing it, because she knows it is not good behaviour. She knows that people would be shocked and angry, and would make her talk to whitecoats about it, but it is the only way (apart from not-eating, or exercising) that she can get some real space in her mind. She would not define herself as a bulimic. Bulimics are sick more often than she is, she thinks. Plus she doesn't binge, no; everything is very restricted and controlled. It is just on the odd occasion, maybe once a month, or sometimes, when things are really bad, then once a week (but that is rare) and she knows it mustn't get out of hand. It is only because she has drunk too much and eaten too much, and it is easy to sort things out in that respect.

Grace doesn't tell anyone this secret. They would think that she was ill again, and that wouldn't be true, would it? Grace smiles to herself, thinking about the extra muesli she might eat as a treat for being such a good girl. The relief she will feel in the morning will be so good in comparison to the aching guilt which attacks her on a normal day. She can even have a big lunch – a really big sandwich – and relax, and just for a minute it won't matter.

She knows she is not alone. Other girls do it, too. They get drunk and they feel ill, and they know how to make it come back up. They even talk about it, but Grace never will. It will sit inside, a secret story of hers, for ever.

Grace lines up at the college canteen. She doesn't often eat there because it means seeing all the cliques of people at their tables, and she feels left out. Grace goes for a jacket potato with tuna mayonnaise. She walks along the queue and pays for it at the till. The girl behind her asks her why she doesn't come to eat in the dining hall more often.

'I do. I do come for dinner. It's just sometimes I prefer to eat on my own.'

'Yeh,' the girl replies looking at Grace's jacket potato, 'but you don't eat proper food, anyway.'

Grace doesn't know what to say. She wants to tell the girl that actually jacket potatoes are 'proper food' where she comes from, but instead she smiles nervously. Grace decides that the girl must have guessed or heard about her anorexia, so she makes sure that she avoids her, because she obviously isn't very nice if she says things like that, which are insensitive.

Grace walks over to the leisure centre with two girls from college. They are going to a heaving Sunday evening aerobics session. Grace hates aerobics because there are so many other girls there, and they are all looking at each other, and trying to outdo one another in the intensity of their 'Heel, toe, knee and change!'

They sit on the floor at the beginning of the class. Everyone is stretching out in their tight lycra leggings and gym tops. Grace is biting her nails. She finds the aerobics session too hard and tiring but she doesn't want to tell her friends. The teacher wears a microphone round her head and she shouts at people. Grace tries to stay at the back of the class so that she doesn't get spotted. She doesn't like shouting. The teacher moves the class around so all of a sudden Grace is near the front. She gets the dance moves wrong because she is too busy comparing the size of her hips with the girls in the front row.

Do they know? Can anyone tell? Grace looks at the panting bodies lying on the floor trying to break through the pain of the sit-ups. Most people, she thinks – most girls – are on a diet or have funny eating habits or go to aerobics three times a week even when they hate it and it hurts, and sometimes it isn't the best thing to do. Sometimes, feeling fat is about guilt and being upset, not about the body at all. So she is not so different after all. They must feel the same as her – better (momentarily) when they are smaller, better (briefly) when they are lighter; when they are less.

Grace prefers doing exercise on her own in the morning, when it is pitch-black and she can feel every muscle in her body. She does not let a week go by without some exercise. That would be impossible. People often tell her, 'You are so good! What willpower!'

This annoys her because it draws unnecessary attention to her body. She would rather people didn't know that she tries to be thin, just in case they guess the real reasons. So she says, 'Oh, no, I don't really do much. I haven't been to the gym for weeks.'

Grace prefers the daytime. In the day she is in control and things run to time. She doesn't like evenings when she is in a club, and she has to drink vodka and Diet Coke in order to feel confident. She keeps drinking and then she makes mistakes. Grace has learned her lesson. She hates dirty, drunken bars, and she hates drunken college boys, and things that happen after too much vodka (they have to be numbed and erased). She hates the way she feels for days after she has had too much alcohol, and the way she can't get the shape of her hips out of her mind. When she gets drunk, things go out of shape. She starts to let go. Everything slips from where she needs it to be. Then she has to block it out and scream inside.

The first term at Cambridge feels like a lifetime. Eight weeks have passed so slowly. Secretly, Grace can't wait to get home. The only part she has enjoyed has been the studying, the hard, eye-squinting, back-aching studying of really difficult books, something that actually challenges her and makes her think, unlike school where it was unacceptable to express this. But on the whole she is pleased that it is the end of term, and that she can stop eating things for show and take back the control. Then she will feel good again. People will be amazed when she comes back next term and looks thin and pretty again. Hopefully they will say, 'Grace looks thin.'

And that will make her feel good.

'Why do you need a hot-water bottle all the time?'

'Grace is always cold.'

'Grace doesn't eat that. Don't put it on her plate.'

'Are you eating properly?'

'You look thin to me.'

Grace goes home for the Christmas holidays. She spends most of the days sitting at a desk studying medieval texts and trying to write essays about things she doesn't really understand. She sits with a hot-water bottle at her tummy. She tells Mum that she has stomach ache. She doesn't want her to think that she needs it. She is cold, because then Mum will think that it is due to her being too thin. Actually, she has put on weight, and some of the old anorexia clothes don't fit any more.

Mum, Dad and family still think that Grace has funny habits. Mum watches Grace sit in front of the fire, knees bent up to her chest, eating her apple. Grace is pleased that she can have a measured-out tomato soup for her lunch rather than big brown-bread tuna mayonnaise sandwiches from the college bar.

Grace feels constantly watched at home, which she finds annoying because now she has her own life, and goes about her days at Cambridge with no one to keep an eye on her and she is, 'Absolutely fine, so there is no need to watch me, OK?'

Grace goes for an early-morning run on the snowy Durham hills. She likes the way it is fresh and freezing. It makes her hands go stiff and her heart beat fast. It is a good feeling, she thinks. If everyone else tried it they might like it too, but they don't. They sit on the sofa and watch TV, and look at her strangely from their warm dressing gowns, eating their toast with marmalade for breakfast.

'I'm back.'

'You must be freezing,' Mum says.

'No, I'm fine. It's really nice out there actually. Anyway, back to work.'

On Christmas Day everything is back to normal. Not like last Christmas when Grace was six stone and dropping, and people were not in any mood to celebrate. This year, things are better, and Grace is at Cambridge University, and mostly the issue is passed over because it is easier that way. Except this year Grace doesn't get any chocolates or sweets in her stocking, and she isn't offered a selection box (so she is given no chance to de-select it). Instead, she gets a bag of dried apricots and some dates. Grace smiles because it is obvious that everyone is trying not to offend her or make her feel awkward. So there are just (correct) assumptions made and things unsaid, unspoken and unopened, which she is happy about because she does not want things to be difficult and awkward (although they are inside).

Grace and family sit around the dinner table. Grace puts two roast potatoes on to her full Christmas dinner plate to show that she is fine, and she sips her Diet Coke quietly, as if its dietness has no meaning. Nobody talks about last Christmas, or last year much at all, or the last version of Grace that went with it. They just pull crackers and wear hats and read out silly jokes, and eat their Christmas dinner in the usual quick way, so that people can get back to what they really want to do – watching TV, reading books, not-eating things. Grace doesn't have any Christmas pudding, instead she has a yoghurt and then spends the afternoon sneaking into the kitchen and picking at the icing on the Christmas cake, but no one says anything. They simply mop up the remnants of the anorexia (the strange food requests, the slightly slim daughter, the order and routine of her). They conceal the spill over, because it is too painful and confusing to do anything else.

PLAY ON

[We see Grace standing outside an audition room. She is shaking with nerves. She grips her bag with both hands. Two girls appear and join her. They open the door to the room and all three go inside. The girls prepare the room, while Grace stands to one side. She kneels down and she pulls some bits of paper out of her bag.]

GIRL 1: Are you ready?
GRACE (OUTSIDE VOICE): Yes, yes I am.
GRACE (INSIDE VOICE): *Get this right, or you will look a fool.*
GIRL 2: OK then, Grace, go ahead.

[Grace looks at the piece of paper and prepares to sing. The lights fade down. As they come back up Grace is sitting in a dressing room, in front of a mirror. She is looking in the mirror and taking off her make-up. She stops and looks at the audience. The audience and the mirror are both facing her.]

GRACE (INSIDE VOICE): *I need to sing and to act. It's the only time I feel good, when I have been on the stage, and people recognize me and make me feel like I am a success. I get space in my head where all I can think about are words and music and everything else is blocked out. I can't hear any other voices. It's an amazing freedom. I'm playing a whole other character and I am allowed to do so. Sometimes it can be an hour or two of being on stage and it is the longest, best hour of my life because I'm not bashing myself about at all, not in any way. Things feel like they are better. I am better.*
GIRL 1: *[Spotlight up on a parallel chair to Grace's – spoken straight to*

the front] Are you coming for a drink, Grace? We're going to the pub.

GRACE (OUTSIDE VOICE): No, no thanks. I'm tired.

GRACE (INSIDE VOICE): *I don't feel confident, you see. Sometimes I just want to be on my own. It's better on my own. I don't want to go out and be sociable because I need to get my head down and work hard and be the best. Of course there are some good days. I got this main part in the university production of* Fame. *It's the biggest thing I have ever done.*

GIRL 2: *[Spotlight up on a parallel chair to Grace's – spoken straight to the front]* Well done, you were great. Really, you were amazing, the best.

GIRL 3: *[Spotlight up on a parallel chair to Grace's – spoken straight to the front]* Fantastic. Brilliant. See, you did it.

GRACE (INSIDE VOICE): *Somehow, I am not sure how, I managed to get myself to the audition. I went at nine o'clock on a Sunday morning because I knew nobody else would get up that early and go to an audition, not students, not on a Sunday. I hoped that I wouldn't have to see any of the other competitors and that things would be easy. It went well. I felt fine somehow, I got this momentary confidence – I felt thin that day, I think. Then the directors invited me to a second audition where I had to hear all the other girls sing, and that was hard because I couldn't be the best. I was mentally shouting at myself. Bla, bla, bla. I wondered why I had gone along. Then suddenly there was a phone call, and they told me that I had got the part and I was crying and screaming.*

[She moves around the stage, gesturing and speaking in exaggerated voices.]

'This is the best thing that has ever happened to me.'
'This is all I have ever wanted to do, to be.'
'This will make things all right'

'*This will change things. It will. A new me.*'

I have decided it will be better if I am thinner, because it gives me that edge of confidence. A little push. I have to wear tight black leggings and leg warmers [she looks down at her outfit] and a leotard on the stage in front of a big audience. So I don't eat my lunch, I just have muesli for breakfast and then bananas and Lucozade in the evenings. This makes things a bit tiring, but it means that I can try and concentrate on my acting, and not the size of my hips. I don't have my periods any more (not for the last few months anyway) but it doesn't bother me, things are a bit easier that way. It's just because I have lost some weight (I think I must have) and they switch off at a certain level.

[Grace sits on the floor.] When I make a mistake in the play, do you know how that feels to me? I have to go home and pull things apart, and then I don't want to go outside any more, or see anyone's face. They will have noticed my mistakes. I know they will. I won't have any muesli the next day because I need to make up for the mistakes by looking the thinnest I can on the stage. It's OK because it is only for a time, and I'm not starving myself (no way!). I don't want to lose too much weight because things go off course when that happens, and I could get into real trouble, although a couple of pounds wouldn't be a bad idea.

[She stands up and walks to the side of the stage where a group of people are chatting.] The other members of the cast get together. They are friends and they get drunk and laugh and swap numbers. I prefer to stay in my own space. I sit in my room and in my costume and in my act. I don't let them in or reveal myself because they might start to figure me out and ask too many questions. One of the girls asked me to audition for her play at the Edinburgh Festival. I performed well in my American accent at the audition. She called me up and said:

GIRL 1: *[holding a phone]* Grace, would you like the part?

GRACE (OUTSIDE VOICE): Yes, definitely, certainly, absolutely, I would love it. *[Grace puts down the phone and then picks it back up.]* No, no, I can't. I'm sorry. It's just not possible. Sorry to let you down. I don't have much money to spend a summer doing acting and er, I need to do some more studying and er, I well . . . I can't do it. Thanks for asking, though. Sorry to let you down like this, I'm just . . . not ready for that. Thanks, anyway. Please still be my friend. *[Puts phone back down.]*

[Curtain closes.]

Nineteen

Grace sits with her friend on the steps to the entrance of Cambridge University library. Grace is smoking her Marlboro Light. The two girls stand up and turn around to the library door, helping each other to their feet, then they collapse back on the concrete steps laughing hysterically in tandem. There are piles of books in plastic bags by their feet. They sit so tightly together that from a distance it is hard to tell them apart. It is only when somebody else enters the frame that their bodies appear to dissolve and Grace is shown to be hiding behind her friend, under the shape of her shadow, in the strong sunshine.

A boy approaches, and Grace's friend stands up and kisses him hello. Grace sits back, leans on her hands and bites the skin around her inner lip. Her friend continues to talk to the boy, Grace looks up and smiles. The boy nods his head towards Grace and then turns back to her friend. Grace sits silently and checks her watch. The minutes are tick-tocking by and she hasn't done any work today.

It is hard having a best friend, because it means that you can't do everything at the exact times you want to, Grace thinks to herself. Grace goes everywhere with her best friend. It is like living a whole different life, away from the one she grew up in. It feels easier that way, to do the things that someone else does. It is good to be able to grasp on to the centre of someone else, to move her forward. But if her friend wasn't there she would have been in the library hours ago, instead of driving around Cambridge, getting a Starbucks coffee and watching her friend eat breakfast.

Grace eats breakfast in the house before she goes out every morning so that she won't be tempted by the food in the library café, which is not what she should be eating, and which wastes valuable revision time. But her friend doesn't feel that way, she isn't as controlled as Grace; it appears that not many people are. Grace knows that people sometimes find her behaviour annoying, with her difficult eating habits and her topsy-turvy behaviour. But her best friend doesn't mind too much, she even finds it intriguing; the way Grace is different from everyone else.

Grace's friend looks at her out of the corner of her eye. 'That's a brave thing to do for Cambridge.' The boy on the steps looks towards Grace.

'Sorry?' Grace hasn't really been listening.

'Your dissertation. What is the exact title?'

Grace feels embarrassed. 'Well, it's something like, *Flirting with Food: Fasting and Feeding in the Brontës' Novels*. Do you know much about the Brontës?'

He does, of course.

Grace continues, 'Have you read Charlotte Brontë's *Shirley*? It begins with a quote from there: "Men of England! look at your poor girls, many of them fading around you, dropping off in consumption or decline."[26] So, yes, that's it, really. I didn't think about it being brave.'

'Oh my God. For Cambridge, yeh. You're talking about eating disorders, right? That's so not a traditional topic, is it?' He flicks his hair.

Grace shrugs her shoulders and looks away from him. She wonders from his comment about her apparent 'bravery' if he thinks that she is bound to be a failure, or if he thinks that she is stupid (most likely, as he is a very clever postgraduate English Literature genius) or, worst of all, if he has guessed her secret. This bothers her for some time. Grace covers her eyes from the sun, from his smile and from his

tilted, peering head and hopes he will forget all about her
and her fixation with all things to do with eating disorders.
Grace wonders if she should never think about anorexia
again, but it keeps lurking. She keeps reading about it or
encountering it in various places even when she isn't looking. She didn't realize it was something that was present all
those years ago, even if it didn't have a name then. In fact,
she hadn't really thought about it in that kind of a univer-
sal way, only really in relation to herself, and now she has
folded it away behind her, she tried not to do that either.

Grace wonders what it would be like if she hadn't become
anorexic, if things would have been different. Maybe she
wouldn't have had such a different-from-her kind of friend.
Perhaps she would have been more confident, sociable or
popular? But she struggles to remember what she was like
before the anorexia took over, what she looked like, or
sounded like, or how she laughed (did she really?).

Grace's mum says to her, 'Why don't you bring your friend
home to meet us? If she's your best friend then we should
definitely meet her.'

But Grace remembers that she can't bring her friend home
because she doesn't want the two worlds to meet. Things
are secret in one world, and not in the other.

The only downside to having one single-focused best
friend is that now the people in college, who she tries to
keep at a distance, think that she is being rude:

'She doesn't like us.'

'She thinks she's above us.'

'She doesn't make any effort.'

Grace prefers them to think that, because it is too hard
to have to make an effort, to reveal herself to them
completely or to join in with their unbalancing student life.
Sometimes she has to go along to dinners and say things
like, 'I think I am allergic to that' or, 'I'm not feeling very

well. I think I have a bad stomach' or, 'I don't have very much money so I won't have the full meal like you.'

She sits at the table and drinks her glass of tap water, and smokes her cigarettes, and plays with her napkin and pretends she is having a good time. She would really rather be alone, sitting at her desk in her bedroom, or reading a book, or thinking about things. It is good to have a lot of time alone, to figure things out, Grace thinks, because nothing the other students say seems to make much sense. Cutting off is just easier. Grace is busy thinking about topics such as how many teaspoons of mayonnaise go into an ordinary shop-bought sandwich, which is not a topic for discussion. And when she has finished with that line of thought, she has to discard the facts she has just learned because she knows that it is 'very wrong' and 'bad' to think like that (like the old Grace, who only cared about fat and calorie contents).

Usually the other students laugh or shout and it makes her feel uncomfortable that she isn't joining in, so she has to concede. They interrupt her plans – she has to eat everything, she has to drink cocktails and wine and eat pizza and puddings. Then it feels like she is scrambling for days trying to get her grip back on things. The whitecoats would be happy with the disruption, Grace thinks. They would be so pleased that things are being taken out of her control. It is not that she doesn't ever want to have fun, but she is just trying to keep things balanced, don't they get it? Can't they try and understand? She doesn't want to have to stand up at the head of the table and say, 'Tonight I won't be having any chocolate cake or any pitchers of creamy cocktail because I have old problems with food and I would rather not eat and drink too much. In case it makes me veer to extremes.'

Because then they would never look at her the same way again. So instead, they talk about work and people she doesn't

know and what they are going to do with their future. Grace
has no idea about her own. Some of the people round the
table have got interviews and jobs lined up. They are all
thinking about the end of university, but Grace is only really
starting to get into it. She doesn't really have any job ambitions. Everything got drained away with the anorexia and it
hasn't come back.

Grace goes to see a career advisor.

'So, what is it you are interested in? What would you like
to do?'

Grace smiles, 'I don't know. I don't really have any ideas
about jobs, not office jobs where you sit all day in front of
a computer and file things. I don't know.'

Grace thinks about her perfect head-dream. In her head-
dream she lives in a clean flat, which has white walls and
bare floorboards. It is peaceful and no one gets in the way.
She has a personal trainer who comes to train her every day,
and a special chef who never lets her eat more than she
should, and keeps her completely in shape. This, she is sure,
is the answer to her problems. As long as she has a flat
stomach and thin thighs then she can forgo everything else.
It's as simple as that.

'So . . .' the career advisor looks puzzled.

'I don't know, maybe I'll be a writer.'

The career advisor is confused. There are no boxes to
check and companies to apply to for that one.

'What about management consultancy or maybe banking?
I can give you a handbook so you can do some research.'

Grace snarls. 'No, sorry, I don't think so. I don't think
that is me at all. I don't think those things fit with me.'

And she realizes that she doesn't even know what those
jobs actually are, or who the 'me' is that she is referring
to.

★

Grace sits on the sofa in her university house. She has finished her final exams and despite a couple of crying fits about papers she thinks she has spoiled, she is feeling OK.

'So . . . how did they go?' a friend asks.

'OK. I don't know. I messed something up. I did OK,' Grace replies.

'You'll be fine. You always do well.'

Grace wants to scream.

Grace picks up the payphone in the station and dials the number. She is taking a break from the coffee bar where she is serving out hot chocolate with cream, and skinny, semi-skimmed or regular caffè lattes to London commuters. She likes it when they order a croissant or cake: 'Would you like something to eat with that?' she asks them. It is amazing how it works, how they suddenly say yes and break their planned control.

She rings her tutor to find out her results. This is everything that she has been waiting for. 'Hello. It's Grace. I am ringing for my results.' She puts the heavy black receiver in both of her shaking hands to try and steady it.

'Well done. You should be really proud. You did fantastically.'

Grace goes home from the coffee-shop job and eats her dinner from the Co-op on her own – pasta and green pesto. Then she walks to the kitchen and places her plate in the sink. She sighs. She thinks of washing it up, but she decides not to. She walks to the fridge and opens the door. She takes out a chocolate bar that she has bought herself for passing her exams and for finishing with university. She bought it on her own, in the shop. Not to impress anyone or to demonstrate she is eating to a worried onlooker, but because she wanted a chocolate bar.

I just feel like eating one, OK?

Grace takes the regular-sized chocolate bar back into the living room with her cup of tea. She decides that she will eat two squares. Two squares become the whole bar. Grace smiles. She hasn't eaten a whole, proper chocolate bar for years. The whole bar at once!

I got here on my own, she thinks, I worked hard. Things don't come easy – I do have to work hard. But I did better than they know. More than they will ever know.

Spillover

A year on from my diagnosis, at the very start of university, I was, from a physical perspective, back into the body that I had left behind. My body was a bit smaller, a bit more fragile, more scarred from the stretch and shrink of my skin, but essentially, to the untrained eye, I was back to normal. I had made a declaration to the world that I was better and that I was no longer in need of any help. In body terms I had made a truly 'remarkable recovery', one that people were mostly happy to believe. I had managed to get things back in order. I got a place at Cambridge University to read English. I was seven and a half stone, maybe eight, maybe even a bit more in my second and third years and I was determined not to slip and let anybody know.

I didn't realize at the time that I wasn't alone with my problems. I was like many other people[27] who experienced problems with food at university or college, even if those problems were not classified or diagnosed as full-blown eating disorders. We did not share our stories, and it is only now, years after leaving university, that I am aware that there were others like me who battled alone with anorexia, or bulimia, or both, but we were all too secretive and too locked in our own self-absorbed worlds to notice.

Bulimia nervosa (recurrent binge-eating and self-induced vomiting or evacuation of food eaten) has a slightly later average age of onset than anorexia (according to different reports, around seventeen to twenty-one years[28]). It was only recognized as a clinical condition in its own right in 1979.[29] It is common for people who have suffered from an eating disorder to swing between both anorexia and bulimia[30] and many anorexics do end up using this method of weight control, even if it is only a temporary measure. My experience of the purging element of this condition was infrequent and it did not last long (to be diagnosed a bulimic, the compensatory behaviour – that is how it is termed – has to be happening 'at least twice a week for 3 months'[31]). But the fact that I was not an official bulimic is irrelevant to the fact that the behaviour was a relapse. It meant that the recovery of my weight – perceived from the unknowing outside to be solved – did not necessarily equate with a full recovery from anorexia. It is likely that at this time I had an Eating Disorder Not Otherwise Specified (EDNOS). This means that I met with some of the criteria for bulimia and anorexia, but did not display all the symptoms. Again, this is something that is common. Anorexics very often do relapse several times, and an average recovery (being free from behaviours) length is around five years.[32] Among those who do recover, a large proportion recover to the extent that they manage the illness in a way that allows them to maintain it to some extent, rather than overcoming and moving on. Getting better involves not only addressing the symptoms of the illness – the eating restrictions – but it also involves exploring the causes of it. This, for me, was to be a separate exercise and one that I could not do in its immediate aftermath in the intensity of university.

It is still hard, looking back on my time at university, to see what I was truly feeling. My Cambridge experience is hazy, almost like the memory got distorted, spun out of shape. I cannot see myself clearly; I cannot hold the memory. Perhaps I filtered it out. I chose to use other pieces of me to make up my identity, rather than the half-felt, half-experienced time in this part of my recovery. There was just a sequence of things, which I needed to achieve. Externally,

I was ambitious, charged, energetic and intellectual. I did not let the fading insides come into show. This was the way it happened and then ended, without reflection or understanding. There was simply achievement and a series of successes and, sometimes, failures.

I did not know how to define myself or what I stood for, and so I looked for things to define me. When people asked me what I wanted to be, I would try and find words and expressions which I felt represented me, but at the same time words which fled from any real commitment to any one thing. I had been running for a long time. I had been unable to make decisions for myself.

'It must be in my genes!' Or, 'It's my star-sign,' I would say.

For too long I let myself believe that this indecisiveness and lack of self-determination was an immovable part of me. I cried at the thought of any real responsibility, or any real allegiance to anything or to anyone. I evaded things I did not want to confront or did not want to do, like I did when I was a little (littler) girl. I let friends down, and I lost contact with people (and they with me) because I did not like to give myself to anything, because I couldn't face the commitment of it. Then, paradoxically, I would suddenly take on something so great, so huge, that it threatened to overwhelm me, almost as if I was making up for all the other things I had failed to stick at or commit to or decide on.

This behaviour seems to be a common theme in those who have suffered from anorexia. Whether it is an associated personality trait, or a reflex of the anorexia itself, to those people with anorexia life often seems to be a set of polarizing choices. There is success or there is failure, there is black or there is white. There is fat or there is thin. Things around them, and the choices they make, are always in opposition. It appears to tie back to that obsessive, perfectionist behaviour that is often a key characteristic. The obsessive behaviour extends beyond the food relationship into other areas of life. As the food relationship begins to normalize it seems to be common for other obsessive tendencies to take over: a need for symmetry, a need for things to be straight, ordered, tidy, neat and controlled.

In the same way as I could be rigidly controlled, I could also veer to the other extreme. I would suddenly offer up myself to something on the spur of the moment. I would make a decision without any thought, I would buy something expensive, I would agree to something I didn't want, in a half-shaded thought. This behaviour was the way of coping with my guilt for having avoided so much. That was the way to tell people that I was in charge and that I seemed to be making rational choices, but actually when my restrictive self was thwarted, my extreme veering self was revealed. I was moving from one polarity to the other with no breath in between.

By the end of university, I was four years away from the start of my illness, and I believed it to be behind me. I wanted so much to be something else, something other than an ex-anorexic. I looked at myself and I thought about how it would be impossible, after university, to go back to the house I grew up in, in the town which had far too much knowledge about me. Instead, I needed something separate, something far away, something new to continue my story. The end of university, like the end of school, was something I couldn't avoid and I simply had to face it, but this time I needed to do it in an adult way. I took it upon myself to invent the next chapter of my story on my own.

In the end, the only real way out of eating disordered behaviour was to turn it round for myself and this is what I did. The desire to get better has to come from the inside, it just has to, and I realize that is a frustrating piece of advice, because in the midst of it, that just seems impossible. But somehow I managed to do it, so I do not think that impossibility is an excuse. It is an excuse you make to yourself because you know it is really hard to break the cycle of anorexia, and you don't want to have to try something so painful and so very difficult. In my spillover period, the reality of this self-healing became clearer to me every day. I realized again that I alone had to fight my impulses to fall back to the easy option of cutting out food or being sick because I felt unable to cope with something.

What became evident was that somewhere along the way I had made the decisions for myself. I was the girl who had decided to restrict her food intake on certain days and not on others. I was the one who had stood in front of the mirror and had chosen to make myself sick when I felt I needed to. I was also the one who had initially decided to go to university and to get out of the anorexia in the first place. Once I knew how self-determining I could be and what a powerful tool that was, I also knew that I had the ability to reject the voice of anorexia outright and all that went with it. This was a hugely important learning.

PART 5

Finding the Edges

Twenty

One day, Grace sits at her desk in her bedroom in her Cambridge house. There is a hot summer stillness which hangs in the air. Results are in, another thing is completed and achieved. Grace can't seem to sit and relax. Things have been so up-tempo and intense for months that to let go would be to collapse. She pulls out a pen and paper from her desk drawer and starts to make a list.

Jobs/things I would like to do next:
~~Actress~~
Can't just 'be' an actress. No money. Can't go to drama school. Can't even get myself to auditions for university play. So no chance.
~~Journalist~~
Made one application and failed. Obviously no good.
~~Go back home and save some money~~
No no no. I can't go back home now. What would happen if I did that? What a stupid idea. No way. I would be going backwards. I would get stuck. I can only go forwards. I wouldn't be able to do my exercises or go for a run without feeling like I was doing something wrong.
Reminder: need to do my exercises! Must go to the gym.
They might start buying me low-fat microwave meals and I would feel like they still thought, after all this time, that I had some kind of issue. It's been three years since I came here. Four years since the label got stuck on me. So no. Anything but. I still can't. Rather get away.

Grace picks up a graduate careers handbook with ideas on different types of jobs and a directory of companies, and she starts to flick through it.

A is for Accountancy

A is for Actuary

A is for Advertising

She stops, and scribbles on her piece of paper, Advertising!

She quickly tears off another piece of paper and starts to write a practice letter:

Dear Sir/Madam,

I am very interested in your company. I am just about to graduate from Cambridge at the end of the month and would very much like the opportunity to meet with you to discuss the possibility of joining your advertising agency.

I look forward to hearing from you.

Yours faithfully . . .

She works through the handbook, crossing off names of companies as she goes. She is frenetic, charged, impulsive. Anything to stop her going backwards, anything to take her away.

She sends letter after letter, each one housing one of her stories:

'This is what I have always wanted to do . . .'

Or, 'I really see myself fitting into your company.'

Or, 'I would welcome the opportunity to show you who I am.'

And, 'I am a hard-working, disciplined and yet creative person.'

She dresses herself in a suit, and she constructs another form around her body. And they ask her, 'Why do you want to work in advertising?'

She answers with the fluidity that never evades her in such

situations. She has the perfect response for all such questions. All worked out. Line-perfect like a perfect actress should. Then there are handshakes and contracts and working hours, and she is going to lead a real life, and put a stop to those ridiculous head-dreams.

Grace sits in her Cambridge living room on the edge of the sofa. She is holding a cigarette in one hand and the phone in another:

'Mum, Dad, guess what? I had an interview! It was in Knightsbridge, in London. I tripped along Sloane Street in my Topshop heels. Usually I am over-prepared for interviews, you know me, but for this one I didn't get a chance. I just sent off a few letters, and then I am there, in this bigger-than-you-can-imagine office block, talking about TV ads. It all happened so quickly. The lady called me back the next day, and she told me that I had got a job! Can you believe it? I got a job, in advertising! It's only a placement to start off with, but I'm going to be working for one of the biggest companies there is. So I'm not coming home. I'm not coming back, not now. I don't know when I will be back, I'm afraid. But you are pleased for me, aren't you? I have made you proud, haven't I? I need to make you pleased and proud, especially after all I put you through. You know, that thing. But that's over now. Look what I've done. I've moved on, we don't have to talk about it any more. Thanks. Bye.'

So Grace packs up her case, locks the door of her Cambridge house and says goodbye to her friend, to university and to the stories that she made there. Just like that.

The first days at work are high-pitched and hot. Grace puts on her new work clothes and eats chocolate biscuits in presentations. She is very careful that no one gets the wrong idea this time, so she is sure not to be fussy or funny when it comes to food. It is difficult because there are sandwiches and crisps on every table. Fat, gloopy sandwiches with globules of mayonnaise seeping out of the sides. And so she keeps hearing the words, *chicken, fat, mayonnaise* over and over in her head on replay.

Grace has got to keep up with her story of advertising ambitions. She falls deeper and deeper into her story and begins to convince herself of its reality more and more each day.

Dear Best Friend,

How are you? Sorry I haven't been in touch but things have been so busy, trying to sort out my new job and make new friends. I can't let myself think about where I was before this. I just have to get on with my new life and put the old one behind me. I'm still trying to find my way around, not like at home where everything is small and clear and controlled. London doesn't seem to work like that.

At work there are a few of us graduates and we are all in competition for a real job. It's a two-month trial and sometimes it all gets very intense. We have to work late and go to the agency bar and be happy and sociable and friendly. There is lots of drinking, but I don't mind because it calms my nerves. Things are blurry, but fun. There is so much noise and busyness that things are quieter inside. I think that I might be enjoying myself – maybe?

Sometimes, though, I feel lost. I am on my own. I don't have any real friends here. I've lost touch with most people – like you. I go home and sit in my room at the top of a house, somewhere on a street that I don't know, in an area that I don't know, in a London that I don't know, and I look out of the window.

I have tried really hard to get here, so I'm not going to

let things turn around. I keep eating and drinking, and making people happy. I haven't let out my secret either because I don't want anybody to know. I let it out too much at university, and it made some people uncomfortable, they always held their distance.

Anyway, everyone has things from their past, and they don't share them out, not when they're over. You don't go on and on about bad things that you experienced because it's totally self-indulgent to do so. You have to get on with life, don't you? You can't be burdened with this kind of thing and you shouldn't burden other people with it. You should be positive, not absorbed in your little eating problems, even if they do still seem like huge, monstrous things.

'Smile, it might never happen.' That's what people say, isn't it, even if it already has?

And it is over. It's a new start. A brand-new me. See you soon maybe.

Love,

Grace

Twenty-one

They meet on the balcony of a tall building overlooking London. She has no idea where she is or how she got there. A group of them got in a taxi after work. They arrived at a party; they drank some wine and laughed and shouted. She joined in. She danced to some salsa music. She danced alone, round in circles, to herself, arms out to the sides, feeling and stroking the space around her. She balanced carefully, swaying back and forth on her high-heeled work shoes. She went outside for some air and he was there. It was unexpected, in the total unfamiliarity of the place, of the time and of herself, to find something so familiar right there, bottle of beer in hand, stepping forward to talk to her.

They go back inside and he dances with her. He spins her around and she collapses into him. He goes to the bar and buys her drinks. She plays with her hair and twists her cigarette between her fingers. They stumble out on to the pavement. He holds her hand, and they walk down the street, across the road, over the traffic lights, past the Tube station. She feels her head go dizzy with the disorientation, the sudden lack of control. He takes her to McDonald's. She decides on a Filet-O-Fish burger. She hasn't eaten a real burger for years and this one comes pretty close. He orders a McFlurry. He offers her a spoonful. She tastes it. It is cold and sweet on her tongue. Ice cream is not on her agenda. She doesn't feel too bad either. The coldness of it is intriguing, the sweetness, powerful.

★

She looks at him over the dinner table. Red wine smudges her pink lips. She talks about her family, about university. He asks her questions. She asks him back. Words float from one side of the table to the other, conversation sails.

'I have a secret,' she says.

He listens.

She looks down at the tablecloth and rubs the side of her ring.

'It's just, I used to have an eating disorder. That's why I am a year behind. Why I had a year off. That's what I did, in that year. I mean, I did work in the pub, that wasn't a lie, but I was also ill. I guess I could have died had it gone on longer.'

Then she stops. She can't think why she did it, why it came out like that, instead of the story with the big gaps that she usually tells. Something made her tell him about it. She eats some more of her big bowl of cheesy gnocchi and smiles at him.

'It was ages ago. It's just, it's a big part of me, so I'm not ashamed of it. I'm over it, and so I can talk about it now. Yes, I need to talk about it.'

She goes to the toilet and wipes the red wine stain from her mouth. She looks in the mirror. *Why did you do that? Why did you let it out? Stupid girl.*

She comes back to the table, she is quick in the bathroom, in case he might be thinking that she is being sick in the toilet. He might think things like that about her now, now she has let him in.

They sit in his flat, late into the evening. She calls him her boyfriend. He seems uncomfortable, but she has no doubt. *Everything will be OK if I am with you.*

She eats the dinner he has cooked for her. She drinks the wine. She smiles and laughs and relaxes and sleeps comfortably, and the intrusive self-thoughts are quiet.

If I am with you then the things in my head go away.

Not an utterance, she realizes. The hours have passed and
she hasn't looked at the clock and tutted to herself for something that she hasn't done.

*Don't make me go back to my flat. Don't make me be on my
own. Not when things are so perfect, so quiet, so different from
everything I know.*

He takes her to meet his family.

'Shall I mention anything about, you know, certain foods
that you don't want to eat?'

He has watched her. Things have crept in, bit by bit. She
doesn't eat desserts in restaurants. She doesn't like fast food.
She asks him about her weight, her shape, her food – a lot.

'No. No way. I'm fine. I'll eat anything. Don't let them
know, will you? Please. I couldn't stand it. I'll be fine. I
would hate it if they knew and judged me. You haven't told
them, have you?'

'Of course not. Don't worry. If you'll be OK, then that's
great.'

She is sure that she will be.

She dresses in her smart work clothes. She wants to make
a good impression, but not a fat one or a thin one either.
In fact, she thinks it will be better not to stand out at all,
if possible, because they will all be looking, weighing up,
deciding.

She takes up the offer of crisps and nuts and dips with
her glass of wine, and another glass.

*Hi, everyone. I am normal. I am nice. Please like me. Thanks
for the food, please like me.*

It is a big family meal round the table. Course after course.
Talking and questions, and traditions, and family jokes. She
thinks of her growing-up house and how things are so
different here, so much bigger, so much louder, so much

more grown up. At home she had tea at five o'clock and usually it was something like shepherd's pie and then apple crumble. They would eat tea on their knees in front of *Neighbours*. It is not like that here, she thinks, the way that people talk about their food, and take time over it, and ask questions like, 'So, do you like garlic?'

And she says, 'I suppose so. I don't know. Yes, yes I do.'

She wonders if there is garlic in the dinner, and so says yes, because it would be a bad thing to be rude, and they might not like her if she sounds fussy.

They ask her if she likes her dinner and she says (without hesitation), 'Yes, it's delicious. Lovely, thank you. Thank you for having me.' Like a good girl should.

They ask her if she wants more and she doesn't, not at all, but she says, 'Thank you, yes, it's delicious. Yes, please.'

They talk about all the different meals they have had, and the different tastes and occasions on which they have eaten things. She doesn't have much to say on such matters because she usually eats in secret, in private, when no one is looking.

He glances at her to check that she is all right. She doesn't want him to make a fuss, and he doesn't. He doesn't know where she has come from, and how different things are there.

Don't guess my secret, please.

She sits on the sofa with his family after dinner (crisps with dips, bread, soup, chicken, potatoes, vegetables, dessert). She eats chocolates with her coffee. People are talking and asking her questions, but all she can feel is her stomach swelling under her tight trousers. She tucks her legs under so that she doesn't have to see them. She asks him for a baggy jumper so that the edges of her disappear.

'Just a bit cold, that's all. Oh no . . . it's not your house that is cold, just me. I'm a bit like that!'

After the meal has ended, they say goodbye and she thinks she has done a good job making people like her.

They sit on the Tube side by side. He looks at her. 'Thanks for coming. You are amazing.'

She closes her eyes and she takes deep breaths and she grips his hand tight.

Grace smiles as she finishes her presentation. She fields their questions one by one. An external confidence oozes. They offer her a permanent job. She has succeeded. She is sure that it is the right thing to do, to put behind her all the childish notions of writing and creativity. Someone like her can't do something like that, can they? How would she earn money? Impossible. Switch it off.

She phones up Mum, to tell her about this new achievement. Mum is pleased, but perhaps surprised – not that Grace has got the job (of course she has) – but that she actually wants to do that kind of thing as a career. Her mum says, 'OK, love, whatever you want to do.'

But Grace knows that Mum worries about her, worries that advertising isn't really what she is about, worries that the corporate world isn't for a sensitive girl from a small place, not for someone who feels things the way she does, soaks them in through her thinner-than-thin skin. Mum worries that Grace won't cope with the pace of life in London because, really, she looks thin and probably she doesn't eat properly, not at all, not by the look of things.

The family come to visit. Grace prepares the itinerary, plans it out so that everyone will have a good time – *please do* – and so that everyone will be happy and pleased with her. But London is noisy and full of people and there is rubbish on the streets. It isn't like the place where she grew up, in safety and quiet alongside the ever-stretching fields. Grace feels bad that they don't like it. She thinks it is her fault if there is too much rubbish and too many people.

They take the bus back to her flat – a room at the top

of someone else's flat – and she sweats and grinds her teeth every time the bus comes to a stop in the heavy-breathing traffic. She knows that they won't be happy with the long, dirty bus journey home from work. She feels like they aren't seeing it in a good light.

If only they had come on a different day and, *Look how far I have come! I have. I have. Please agree. Times have changed.*

They go to a pizza restaurant and everybody likes the pizza, and Grace has a salad (a big one).

I don't eat pizza, OK? No thanks, not even a mouthful.

She drinks some white wine to stop the guilty feelings, and then she says, 'Maybe you would like to meet my boyfriend?'

They seem pleased to do that, if she is pleased to do that, and they are all pleasing each other. They smile, and she thinks that perhaps they can see the difference in her after all. Perhaps the very fact that she has a boyfriend makes them think of her in a different way, with the anorexia now firmly behind them.

Then they leave, and Grace misses them, and she sits in her room and she wishes she was at home, with the sound of their voices rising up the stairs towards her small bedroom, in her growing-up house.

Twenty-two

He takes her to Borough Market. It is Saturday morning and it is crowded. They are jostled from one stall to the next. From fresh bread to cakes to meat to hot homemade meals served in small tubs, steam floating out into the chilled London air, dark chocolates and creamy coffees. On the edges of the market, the burger, chips and kebab stands, which cross with the organic health foods, sit stall by stall, side by side.

They taste bits of food on cocktail sticks, they buy hot bread, they eat it from the paper bag. They sip mulled wine, gasping for heat through their woolly gloves. After a lovely morning, they jump on the bus home, food nestled under their arms.

They sit in front of afternoon TV, watching the football results come in. Grace tries to concentrate, but unfortunately she has her usual thumping head along with her strong-beating heart, framed with an edge of panic. She did have a lovely time in the market and she enjoyed sampling the food, and she didn't feel too bad at the time, but afterwards, when they got home, she thought about the mulled wine, the olive bread and the pieces of chocolate for hours and hours. And still, here, the inside voice remains, and that is her difference from everyone else: the intoxicating guilt, the sitting, preying guilt.

Grace sits at her desk, early morning in the open-plan office. A girl comes in, past her desk, backpack on, red-faced after a six-mile run to work; she does it every day, every night.

Grace thinks about her own Tube-crowded journey, and looks down at her legs. The girl opposite her desk is on a detox diet, and the one behind her seems to eat only fruits and salad. At lunchtime there are endless streams of people going out jogging around the park.

The office seems to be bursting with the sound of ripping Slimfast tins and low-fat Shapers sandwiches. Grace puts her head down and tries to concentrate on responding to her emails. It doesn't help that she works on the advertising for a cereal company. One of her first challenges was to do a competitive analysis. They sent her out to Tesco, and asked her to buy a box of nearly every cereal on the shelf. She brought them back in a taxi, and lined the boxes up in a row. They told her to taste them all and read the product information so that she would be the expert on cereals and know what each product offered compared to hers. She bought some paper bowls and sat in a room, alone, pouring out small bits of each cereal from the packets, covering them with milk and eating each one. She did it in one afternoon, just because they were there, and she was nervous and intrigued, and because someone gave her an instruction to eat them; things she would never usually touch. She pretended that her bosses would be angry if she didn't try them all. They didn't even ask her about it afterwards. They had more important things to do (it wasn't necessary for them to know how soggy, crunchy or sugary the other cereals were), not realizing they had given her the most difficult simple task of them all.

Now Grace stores all the leftover cereal in the cupboard behind her desk. Lots of girls in the office come to get their lunch from this secret supply.

'I haven't got time to eat a sandwich,' they say.

'Sure, yes, please take some,' Grace replies. But she knows exactly what they are doing. They are dealing with the guilt from last night's dinner – secret-eating, restricting and restraining themselves, while no one is looking, except her.

Another task her bosses give her is to research the newest, faddiest diets. This is very important to understanding how women are thinking, and how they are responding to different foods. A cereal with a slimming claim is one with huge potential, given the nation's interest in losing weight. Women want this kind of information, they all want to know how to lose a few pounds, don't they? It all comes from the celebrity thing – wanting to look like Kate Moss or Jennifer Aniston. This is their insight. The near all-women advertising account team talk it through. It is all about the experience of other women in other places, never themselves, and never their own private eating worlds.

Finding out about diets is not a hard task. Grace realizes that she knows about all of the diets that she finds, or that anyone mentions. When they say to her, 'I've found out about another one – the Caveman diet. Shall I give you the information?' she pretends that she has never heard of it. She lies.

'Oh yes, great, thanks. What's that about then?'

She doesn't want it to seem like she pays any attention to that kind of thing. She will do anything to make sure that her little secret isn't revealed.

She never joins in with their office conversations.

'Did you know that an avocado has more fat in it than a Mars Bar?'

'I'm on a detox. I'm not eating wheat or dairy or meat, and no alcohol and no coffee either. I feel really good. Everything is more in line. I just feel more in control.'

'I'm only eating 1,500 calories a day.'

Grace sits silently in the corner and eats her sandwich. She ducks beneath the sounds of their voices talking about the gym, Atkins and what they haven't eaten for breakfast. She makes loud noises on her keyboard.

Tap, Tap, Tapity, Tap, Tapity Tap, TAP TAP.

She smiles and pretends that she is not interested. She is sure that they are looking at her differently. Sometimes people say things like, 'You've lost weight' or, 'That salad looks very healthy.'

She stumbles over a few words, paranoid about every half-comment about her weight and size and what she is eating (no matter how nondescript, no matter how much it was just something to say to pass the time). Still she keeps it inside. It is locked up tight, and no one will get to know her secret plans.

Eventually it becomes impossible not to at least try the diets. She tries them for a couple of days. She does the detox, the Atkins, the 'drop a dress size'. She does them all, briefly, but she knows that she is not supposed to. She knows that they are a triggering action. She knows that it means that something else is·wrong, not her weight, not her shape. Something is revealed at the start of every new decision to do more exercise, to drop a pound. Something starts clicking in her head, and she decides to sit down and try hard to work it out.

Grace picks up a women's magazine in the corner shop. It always happens like this; she sees the front cover and there is a reference to, 'My secret eating disorder' or, 'How anorexia ruined my life.'

She feels compelled to read them. It is scary to think that some part of her is obsessed by these articles, even though she wouldn't do anything to purposefully resurrect her eating disorder. It is as if her brain is programmed by anorexia to search out the relevant information, to filter it through at super-speed and she can't seem to lose the ability to do it. In these confessionals, there is rarely a picture of the survivor involved in this shameful secret; sometimes they even use a different name to protect their identity. Grace wonders why this would be the case, and why they are made to feel like they have done something terribly wrong. She checks that the article looks interesting and then quickly goes to the counter and buys it. She certainly doesn't want anyone to think she is buying it for *that* reason. Oh no, she is buying it for the fashion, for the celebrities, not for the eating disorders, they are something that one must lock away!

The worst thing is that the authors say things like:

'It never leaves you.'

'Oh yes, it is always a part of you – you can never switch it off completely.'

Grace doesn't want to believe that. Why do people feel satisfied with that answer? Grace's guilt and fear are ever-present and they move things in ways that restrict her; they stop things happening in her life, they close things off. She can't possibly let herself imagine that it will always be this way. She closes the pages of the magazine article. She will have a better ending than that in her story, she thinks, but there is perhaps some way to go before she can get there.

PART 6

What Shape Am I?

Twenty-three

Sometimes I wake up and I can't remember where I am, or how I got here. It feels like I fell asleep at home and then woke up hundreds of miles away with no explanation. I was inside my world, and then I decided to remove myself from it. I couldn't cope. I wandered about for a few years following whoever would lead me. It hits me when I least expect it. I am standing in my flat and I am looking at my things: my clothes, my furniture, my space, and all of a sudden I wonder why I am not at home with my family. Then I realize that I will never be there again. I am myself, on my own. I have grown up. I have to go to work and be responsible and move forward, not run away. That is it – over. There is no going back to being a girl. It just takes a while to reorientate, to pull myself together and to focus. I am supposed to be having a great career, wanting to get promoted – a successful young woman – so that people will be able to say:

'Look at what she has achieved.'

'She's doing really well for herself.'

That is what you are supposed to do, I think. That must be why I went to Cambridge. That must have been what I was trying to do at school, before other things took over. I can't remember what I wanted to be. I remember the question, 'What do you want to do when you grow up?'

I always had lots of answers – lots of ideas and I was going to do them. Now I sit at my desk behind my computer all day – this is where I have ended up – and I can't stop thinking about how much I have changed. I eat like a normal person, but I don't feel normal inside. The feeling of being fat, and big, and bulky sits on my body and rings through my brain. There is a loud voice always shouting at me: *Stop eating. Hide away. Go back to your quiet head.*

At least I have someone to talk to now, who doesn't mind if I don't want to eat certain things. He just says, 'OK baby, if you really don't want to, but try if you can.'

Something stops me from self-starving. I don't want to do that any more. It just means that it is tiring listening to, and then ignoring, the voices. Sometimes I just can't keep my heart in its place, and it creeps upwards and outwards. I can't hold in my tears. They seem to seep out of my eyes when I am least expecting it, in a shop or on a bus. They start to fall, and I haven't asked them to. All the things I kept inside are now starting to overflow.

I know what the whitecoats would say. I can hear it in my head. They would speak to me in a warm putty voice, 'You are using food as an emotional crux. You are eating and not eating according to how you feel. It is all about your feeeeeeeeelings. How do you feel? How are you today?'

I feel like I have been bashed in the face with my feelings, that is what. All of a sudden I can feel again. All I used to feel was fat, fat, fat. Even when I was all bones and skin and I could see that I wasn't really fat, not in the medical sense of the word, I still felt it inside. But now how I feel about my shape changes every day:

Thin-shaped
I feel thin-shaped when I have cut down on something – maybe alcohol or chocolate. On these days I can wear anything and I can do anything. I am not scared. It's an amazing sense of liberation because I can even eat chips on days like these. I go clothes shopping, or miss a day at the gym, or I change my patterns.

Sometimes I get embarrassed because I feel thin-shaped and I think people are giving me odd looks. I have to eat a big sandwich or meal in front of them so that they know I am normal.

Sometimes they comment without realizing (about my thinness).

'You're OK, you're thin. It's easy for you,' they say.

'Look at you, nice and thin.'

'What are you? About a size ten or something like that, lucky you!'

It makes me uncomfortable. I try and point out my fat bits. I tell them that I am actually bigger than they think, I laugh it off, I try not to react or I act like it is totally normal; that they would think I am thin, of course, because it is the way I have always been.

I have been made to believe that thin-shaped is bad and I should hide it. When I go to the doctors because I have a cold or something, it is evident that they know things about me. It flashes up on their computer screen like a big red alert, 'Anorexia nervosa'. I have to explain that I am an ex-anorexic (in case they need to know), not a present, current one. Then I want to close my mouth. I want to STOP IT UP so it can't tell on me any more.

I don't look too thin, do I?

I am normal, you know. You couldn't tell, not if I didn't tell you about it.

If I'm sick when I have been too drunk, that also makes me feel thin. I don't make myself sick any more, but sometimes I drink too much when I am out with my friends, and my body can't handle it, just like anyone else and I am horribly ill. I pull on some trousers the next day, and I feel great. Even if I have eaten a big, fatty meal in a restaurant where you can't measure things at all. It's all about the feelings, you see. One day of food has gone from inside, and I feel like a different person. That's just the way I feel.

Fat-shaped

Get dressed. Fat trousers. Reflect on imperfection. Screw up face. Lots of inside shouting. Frame thoughts, and spin them inside my tumble-dryer head. Come out overheated. Fear failure. Mentally slap self about. Try harder. Be smarter. My heart beats in my mouth.

I look down on myself, and all I can see are big shapes. I look in every mirror from every angle. Things look big and out of proportion. I feel like I can't do anything. I am tied up tight inside. I can't focus on the day. I sit at my desk and wriggle in my chair. I make some new resolutions. I go on the Internet and look up some diet plans. I don't like my clothes. I don't get out of my pyjamas, so that I don't have to see my body at all; I don't even have to spend two seconds with it. I close my eyes when I go to the toilet. I switch the lights off at all times. I get some photos out and spend minutes looking at each one, working myself out, checking out the dimensions. I bite my nails. I drink water. I chew gum. I run everywhere. I go to the gym and hurt myself. Just little things like that.

I get under my blanket and things are OK. I am OK. I just need to be at home, by myself, to make things balanced again. I lie on the sofa and I work things out and calm down. I make things calm. I start to think things through. I cancel my arrangements because I can't be with people when I am fat-shaped. Otherwise my balance slips, and I am left in this self-punching mode for a couple of days. It is just too much to take. Sometimes I am just not that strong.

Child-shaped

I'm small and I am scared. Super-anxious. Everything frightens me: the bus journey to work, the traffic on the streets, the people around me, the things I might have done wrong, the planes flying over my head, the Tube stuck in the tunnel, strange streets, strange places, strange people. I am allowed to feel like this, I think. Anorexia is my security blanket: I wrap myself up in my past and that is why I can't face things; it's hard for me, too hard. 'You don't understand, OK?' I cry, and then I go home and curl up tight in a ball and escape the outside world, which might tell me that I have failed, or make me confront my anxieties. I'm like a younger version of myself. I daren't speak to my mum or dad in case I fall back into my childhood tones. I don't want to do that, not again.

Controlled-shaped

Must get to the gym at twelve thirty. Eyes at clock, eyes at screen. Clock, screen, clock, screen. Time barely moves. Twelve twenty-five. Clearing desk. Open bag. Clearing throat.

'Just grabbing lunch.'

Don't tell them that I'm off to run, lift, crunch, sweat. Quick change. Exact routine. Control muscle. Control mind. Body pounds. I feel grounded, whole, secure. Get rid of the inner noises, which need to be drowned out. It makes me feel complete when I bash away at the machines. It is a secret thing. Prepare lunch thoughts. Strut straight to shop. Salad and salmon – look at oil coverage. No pasta – avoid at all costs. Same shop each day, every day. In the queue, all in order. Go home, tidy the flat. Straighten the towels, clean all the surfaces (not a speck of dust!), line up the paper. All straight and secure, all fine.

Out-of-a-shape

I walk up and down, and up and down the aisles of the
supermarket. I don't know what I want. I can't make anything
out. I keep my head down so that no one can spot that I
might be in a bit of a panic. I don't know why I am in a
panic. When I was ill, I knew exactly what I would eat and
what I wouldn't eat, and now I'm not so sure. It changes
from week to week, depending on how I am feeling.
Sometimes I don't eat wheat, or then dairy, or then I read
something about carbohydrates, fish or meat and I change.
I take it all in. Still. I scan the magazines for all the latest
information. I do make sure I eat enough, though. I never
under-eat. I wouldn't dare any more. I wonder what it might
look like on CCTV cameras when I have been walking up
and down the aisles for ten minutes and I haven't picked up
a single item. I spot some sushi and I think that would be
nice but it's not what a normal person has for their dinner,
is it? Maybe it is, I don't know. I put it down, and then I
pick up some chicken, and some stir-fry, but then I had a
big lunch so I don't want to eat something too big. I put it
down. I walk round a bit more and start to feel all panicky,
like I won't find anything that I want. Not here. Not today.
I am starting to quick-breathe as if there is no air in my
lungs, and then I start to pull at my hair because things aren't
going to plan. The inside shouting starts really loud and so,
because I am not concentrating, I bump into a woman, who
rolls her eyes. I decide, that is it. I pick up a carton of orange
juice and walk to the checkout. I pay for the orange juice,
and I run out of the shop, and run run run for the bus
home. The bus sits in traffic and I just want to get home so
I start to sigh and shuffle in my seat. I just want to get home
and look in my cupboards and decide what I am going to
eat because then I will be settled and things will be peaceful and quiet.

When I get off the bus I run run run home.

I take out a box of organic no sugar/no wheat cornflakes from the cupboard and pour myself a big bowl. I sit on the sofa and eat them without looking up, and then I walk back to the kitchen and pour myself another big bowl and repeat. It is dinnertime after all. I walk to the sink and get myself a pint of water. I gulp it down. I walk back to the sofa and sit down. The cornflakes with milk and the water are sloshing around in my stomach. I pull my legs up to my chin and cross my arms. I sit. I sit. I dream it away. Inside there is shouting about the bloating and the sloshing and the volume of cornflakes, but I tell the voice, 'Leave me alone. It's done. I'm done with it.'

I put on the television and I lie down with a cushion under my head, and I turn the television up loud.

I am all these different shapes within the space of a week, and I know that I haven't lost or gained any weight, not an ounce. I know this. I know this now, over and over.

GAME ON

Now its time to restart the game.
  BANG.

Rules:
Don't let anyone find you out
Don't let them break you down or make you confess
Be straight and simple and above all keep up the act
Are you ready?

1. Survive the role of a perfect, successful advertising agency graduate

Sit still. Now you have a job, you need to push things under. Learn how to set up a meeting room. This involves meticulous detail and is well-suited to those with controlling behaviours. When the pens are lined up then everything is in order. Each chair must be at the same height. Each paper pad must be placed in a straight and perfect line. All equipment must be tested and retested. There is no margin for error in this organized, faultless environment. Check and recheck that the air-conditioning system is working. Listen out for any noise which might interrupt or interfere with this very important meeting. Just keep everything in order.

Check, check, check! Now leave the room in its perfect symmetry and return to your desk. Sit by your phone and wait for any possible problems. Always make sure that you shoulder the blame for any issues with machinery, coffee mis-pouring or photocopying blunders.

'You're very good at this,' they say.

'You are so organized,' they remark.

Eat sandwiches at lunch from the canteen. Sit by your desk for as many hours as they need, in front of your computer screen, and don't go home. Eat takeaway junk food late nights and drink beer at your desk and pretend this is, 'Absolutely fine!'

2. Don't let them know that things are getting misaligned

Think of the bathroom silence and run to the toilets. It is safe in the toilet. You can put your head in your hands, and let the tears trickle down your face, and get angry and grit your teeth, and wipe your nose. Make a face. Sigh as you walk towards the mirror, and blame everyone else for making you set up a meeting room, and answer the telephone, and do the photocopying, and get angry in the back of your throat. Don't spit it out, though. Things are blurry and you still have to go back into the meeting room, pick up the pens, place your perfect paper, talk to the builders, run up three flights of stairs to get some fresh coffee, walk into a meeting of twenty people and fix the video. And in your head, where things are all out of shape, you are thinking, 'I didn't survive for this.'

3. Keep up the act when things go wonky-shaped

After the crying and sad faces, agree to do something about this. You need to throw people off course. It will be easier if you at least pretend that you would like some help. Just make sure that you keep them all at a distance. Listen to your thumping-hard heart as you remember that you said you, 'will definitely go and see somebody'.

It was a mistake to say it, but now you need to make things straight again.

4. Smile through it

Smile as you spill out your story to a personnel lady who hands you a clump of tissues. Tell her about your old eating problems and how things are unhappy, now the feeling is back in your body. Smile with embarrassment. Say sorry. Say thank you. This is really embarrassing. She thought you were going to say that you were pregnant. She looks relieved. Imagine hard what that would be like and how, if you did get pregnant, it might mean that you wouldn't have to go to work. Think of all the nice attention you would get, and how people would be happy for you, and send you presents. Think how you could stay at home and stop being ordered around. Snap back into reality and listen as she makes you an appointment with the company doctor.

This is not how it is meant to be. How did I get here? Why am I telling her this? Why did I bring myself to this, when I have been fighting to get away from it?

5. Play along with/play with the professionals

Arrive at the company doctor. Can you see his serious and attentive face? Don't cry too much, but just enough, so he will take you seriously. Listen to his half-hour of advice:

'From my experience, it is advisable that you don't eat some types of foods because they can trigger your manic "up and down" feelings. So I think that you should cut out white bread and sugar. They give you immediate highs and then sharp lows. Does that make sense?'

He actually says you should avoid some foods. Please take

this advice very seriously. Any food reduction is welcome. Say thank you.

Oh, yes please. Thank you, nice man. A real reason not to eat some foods. I knew I should be eating less. I was right. Thank you.

Also make sure you take the anti–depressants he offers for your wonky-shaped unhappy feelings. You are worthy of these pills, which must mean you have a proper problem. No one ever gave you anything like this when you were starving. There is something physical that may be able to be fixed. Then nod quietly when he tells you about the psychotherapist.

Oh no no no no no. Please no more whitecoats. Just some pills, which might make me feel happy and better. I don't understand. I am over things like that. With foods. I 'had' an eating disorder; I don't 'have' one. I told you, remember? I told you about how I got better, and went to Cambridge and was a great success and then came to London and got myself a proper job and made everyone so PROUD of me. They are so pleased with me. I can't tell them that I have slipped. More secrets. More whitecoats. More funny looks from caring people. No no no no no.

6. Play the good girl
'OK, then, Doctor.'

Watch the doctor as he flicks through his notes. Make sure you say thank you. Go on.

Twenty-four

When I arrive at the house of my new whitecoat there is a woman walking out of the door with tissues in her hand and a wet, reddened face. I wonder what story brought her here and who she is seeing. I stare at her tissues and her wet, red face and wonder why I don't react like that when I see the whitecoats. Perhaps if I gave up some tears or some tissues, then they would think things are better and leave me alone.

This time, I have ordered the whitecoats in myself. I almost asked for their help, and so there is a conflict between something I think I must need and something I have avoided time after time. I mustn't let things slip, or let her say or do too much to change me.

I go up the stairs and sit in a clean, richly wallpapered, green room. Things are warm and homely. There are no plastic chairs here. My Chelsea psychotherapist lady is Spanish, and she is beautiful and slim. My whitecoat is sparkling in her designer suit. She asks me how I am. She looks interested and engaged. I can't think why she would be so interested in me. I remind myself that I am better, and ask myself again why I am here.

'Fine. I'm good, thank you. I'm fine. Thanks for asking. Yep, thank you,' I state. 'Thanks for asking.'

There is silence. She doesn't react too well to my pleasantries. I want to puncture the air which is expanding between us. I hate silence and stillness, but my lips are locked and my chest is stiff and I start rolling my eyes around the room to search for some kind of distraction.

I spy with my little eye, something beginning with . . .

She does not break my silence. How long are we going to sit here? She continues to breathe calmly and smile, and she looks right at me.

something beginning with w . . .

What do you want me to say? I think. I'm not sure what I should say. I do feel fine today. I feel OK, honestly. I didn't though, not then, not when I was crying at work, or on that particular night or that forgettable day, but now I am here and I do feel OK. But I don't say it out loud because I am scared of her.

'What do you want to get out of these sessions?' She looks at me carefully, trying to work me out.

I don't want to answer her now because she has annoyed me, I'm not sure why. I get embarrassed when people try and break me down. I would much rather it was the other way. I feel like she is testing me, pushing me and trying to tackle me from all sides.

'Are you angry?' she asks. 'Why have you been feeling like this? How did you get here? What about the beginnings? I would like to know. Can you tell me?'

But I don't really feel anger, I just don't. I don't get hot or fiery, not much. I float in the air, placate, make things nice and I try to make people happy.

'My childhood was happy,' I tell her. 'My family are wonderful and supportive and loving. I really don't think that it is to do with the beginnings. I wasn't pushed or made to feel like I had to do these things. I was always like this. It's just me.'

'So you don't feel angry with your parents for things? Most people do,' she advances.

Now I feel like I am choking. What is there to blame them for? This is no one's fault.

Please don't blame anyone. Please don't put any blame on to

*other people. This is entirely my fault. I was made like this, or I
made myself like this.*

I tell her something with my teeth gritted. I tell her something that I am feeling because I think that is what she wants
to know.

'I'm annoyed at work. I'm frustrated with the photocopying and the tea-making and the smile-wearing.'

'But it's not about the work, is it? The work is not the
real feelings. How are you really? What have you eaten today?
How are things going with food? Do you still struggle sometimes?'

Her Spanish accent rolls off the tip of her tongue and her
words land in front of my face.

I can't believe she mentioned it.

Please don't mention it. I didn't think you would.

'That is FINE. Fine. Everything is under control now.
This is not the issue. I have got over that. I put on weight.
I got better. I eat everything now. I'm not even that fussy
any more. I promise. It's just that now I eat what people
want me to, I don't have anything to project things on to
when I'm a bit out of control, so I get down sometimes. I
have lost the thing that made me feel high; anorexia took
me above any worry and made me feel like I was removed.
That's all. Why do we always have to go on and on about
feelings and thoughts? That is all I do, all day. I think and
over-think. My head is whirring like a food processor and
it hasn't got me anywhere.'

Then there is silence again. I have given her my theory
and she has given me hers. And there is stalemate.

I go every week and we sit. Sometimes she tells me that
I have actually lost weight, which I think is irrelevant. I
can't/don't/won't agree, and I don't like the way she is looking at me and thinking like that. She is actually taking up
one of my evenings, when I could be at the gym running

on the treadmill after indulging in biscuits and fatty sandwiches and wine.

She tells me to close my eyes, and try to relax, and to
take deep breaths because I am stressed inside, but I stare at
her perfect legs and wonder what kinds of exercises she does
to keep them like that. All of a sudden I am here being
asked old questions and feeling like I want to remove myself
from this scene as well.

Silence continues.

I need to say something. I feel like I am letting her down.
I don't want to sit here for much longer like this, leaving
work early to see her. It doesn't feel right any more. I don't
want to be in this place, not now.

She looks at me, and she smiles.

I take a deep breath.

She looks at me and says, 'Why don't you make some
changes to your life? Do something you really want to do?
What do you think about that? You shouldn't be afraid. If,
as you say, this work isn't for you then take the creative path
you have always wanted. I know you have the talent.'

I nod quietly. How can she possibly know that? I don't
want to disappoint her but I know that I would never allow
myself such dangerous exposure. What if I failed? What if
I tried and someone passed judgement and told me I was
no good? How could I cope with reality then? The head-
dreams would melt and I wouldn't be able to get to sleep
any more.

'What things are stopping you?'

I sit and I smile. 'Nothing. Nothing. It's a good idea,
thanks.'

And so she asks me again and every week I reply,

'You are right, it's a good idea. You are right.'

Voice

That is the odd thing about anorexia: it is seen to vanish when the body is mended. It moves from body-side to inside, and perhaps it is more dangerous when it cannot be seen. What may start off as a panic button for a fear about growing up and leaving home, and about having to be perfect in everyone's eyes, turns into a chemical addiction to food. That addiction continues even after it has been beaten on a physical level, because mending your relationship with food does not equate with mending your own self-esteem.

As I started to return to food, and to my body, I became hypersensitive. I felt things from the outside. I could feel other people around me with a strange intensity: I could sense the surge of the crowd, the breath of a stranger, the whirring noise of the traffic. Normal daily events seemed to be enhanced and magnified. As an anorexic, my senses were numbed, nulled and restrained, and then I jumped straight back into the busiest, noisiest world, which initially overwhelmed me. I took it all in with equal intensity, especially other people's views of eating disorders. These were things I hadn't been able to hear before, and it was if they were now magnified, these conflicting voices about what I had suffered, and how it related to the fabric of our society.

Perhaps the most intriguing element of eating disorders and the one thing which it is common to overhear, on a bus or in a shop or in a busy café, is about how impossible they are to understand:

'I don't get it. I mean, I would never think like that. I can't even get my head round how it starts. You eat. You are born to eat. It's one of the only things that you need to have as a human to survive. It's something from birth. It's not like alcohol or drugs or cigarettes – addictions like that come later – you start them, you start to drink or smoke one day, but this one, it's like fighting something elemental. Eating, like sleeping or waking or moving, is natural, it's innate. It starts from in the womb. Why can't they just eat? They should stop being so vain. All that self-obsession is boring. I don't even know how that kind of chain of thinking begins.'

Alongside this, there is, paradoxically, the permanence of the other voices, which are constantly dealing with issues on the perimeter of anorexia: the dieter's voice, the dieting industry's voice, the Government voice, the food guilt, which the whole of society seems to be consumed with. In the small and insular world of a Cambridge college, driven only by the potential success of my next result, I was mostly able to evade it, or maybe I blocked my ears. Dieting just didn't seem to be a topic of conversation – it wasn't mentioned because we were at Cambridge University to be strong and successful women, not diet-obsessed girls. Coming out of the shelter of university, things changed and I was thrown back into the centre of it.

As a society our relationship with food is seen to be out of balance. Obesity rates are rising; we are – apparently – what we eat. When you are in recovery from an eating disorder the magnitude of this voice is often stronger than your own internal one. You have trained that internal voice over time to *Just be quiet and leave me alone.*

But it is all too ready to be convinced otherwise. It is ready to hear all of the food restraints and plans presented by the outside world. It is hard to think that you are an exception to the rule, that you actually shouldn't be going to the gym every day and reducing your calories, or trying the latest celebrity plans. This is what everyone else seems to be doing and why shouldn't you? It is difficult to ignore the verging-on-hysteria of a nation gripped by its size and its shape and everything related to it.

The thing to realize is that a super-controlled relationship with food and body weight will not solve everything. It is a fallacy to believe that happiness comes flooding in on the lighter side of eight stone. I could see that every time I picked up a new diet. It was a symptom of something else. It was a symptom that I wasn't feeling right – and trying to find what I was about through food, like everybody else seemed to be doing, wasn't the answer. I had been there before.

The Passage of Time

The passage of time is a powerful thing. When people ask how you overcome an eating disorder it doesn't sound like the most convincing of explanations to put it down to just waiting for things to get better, but this was the case in my experience. It was a slow process to wear it down but the more I fought it, the more I wanted to rid myself of its strangling hold, and eventually, with sustained effort, the eating disorder voice gradually faded out. As with anyone growing up, things change and develop and move on. In my case, living constantly with such a throttling addiction was very tiring and over time I decided to move away from it, importantly for my sake and not for anyone else's.

A big part of my recovery came down to actually embracing change rather than opposing it. Beneath the chop-change of emotion based on body size, I was bored by permanently thinking about eating and not-eating. I was bored by the frustrating obsession with every inch of my body. I had had enough. Going round in circles over a growing-up issue seemed to be distinctly non-adult. In my early twenties, trying to forge a connection with myself as an independent adult and lose the remnants of my teenage self was an important goal and I wanted to reach towards it. If you are able to admit real responsibility for what you can achieve – if you can start to counter that fear – then you realize that anorexia is something you can put a stop to. I didn't need it to be a part of my life. I needed to find a new shape without it but, importantly, without pretending it never happened.

That is not to demote such a serious addiction to 'just one of those phases'. I don't think it is. The strength of anorexia is such that its remnants are clearly felt, or translated into something else long after the 'phase' has passed. The memory of it is imprinted upon you; it threads through you. It is not something that you forget you experienced. You cannot do this because the potential long-lasting consequences for your body range from infertility to osteoporosis to the erosion of tooth enamel. And it can come back. Even if the relationship with food recovers, the relationship with your body and with yourself can remain a fragile one. But my experience is that recovery is a possibility if you allow it to be, and work hard at it. It will be different for everyone.

The process of my getting better, as I look back, did come in a series of thoughts, or moments. The arrival of my boyfriend is one of those instances. I was suddenly pulled away from the control I thought I had over my life, my body and the foods that it ate. The presence of my boyfriend filled the absence left by the fading relic of my anorexia. It had left me feeling absent. Everything I had known about myself was bound up in my relationship with food. Now I had a new relationship.

Ultimately, the result of the relationship was that I was determined to lock out the anorexic tendencies; and I had found someone that this was worth doing for. He was more fulfilling and more full of potential than any diet was. Momentarily, I stopped caring. I was really determined that I would end this. I would make my relationship work without it.

I do think that things can change, if you are able to sustain a real and lasting relationship outside the one you have with food. Some psychiatrists might say that the ability to have a long-term relationship marks the beginning of the end of an eating disorder. It can open up a new way of living, which begins with 'we' and not 'I'. 'I' is slim and controlled and sharp, from the form of the letter, to its sound, to all that it means. And if this can become 'we', then 'I' gets thrown out of control. In my case, this meant I had to face my fears and confront things that I didn't want to. I think this is important; instead of continually striving for further self-analysis and self-obsession I directed my energies to someone else. It also meant that I could no longer structure and shape every minute of my day just the way I wanted it. I had to battle with my anxiety.

The presence of a relationship meant that my eating disorder voice was disturbed; it became very disturbed when someone else was constantly there with me. And with its demise came hope, and the slow realization that one day the voice might altogether forget to wake up with me, especially when there was someone else who loved me and supported me, and who I loved, waking up with me instead.

The Shape of Emotions

'It's gonna hurt, now,' said Amy. 'Anything dead coming back to life hurts.'

A truth for all times, thought Denver.

Beloved, Toni Morrison

As you recover from very low weight and self-starvation – as you put on more weight, and return to the target you are told to achieve – lots of things do improve (perception can shift and rational decisions can begin to be made), but at the same time it can be a terrifying experience. The biggest change for me was the emergence of real feeling. I felt, like many others who regain weight and grow, that I was thrust back into my hypersensitive body. Emotions returned with full force after a long period of nullification. I went from emotional paralysis to a sense of being flooded with fear and feeling. It was as if all of the experience of the last few years had been unlocked and released, and I was initially totally knocked down with it. The first thing that an anorexic looks to do with that intense emotion is to relate it to her size and weight. She believes this is what shapes all of her feelings and moods, and fuels her happiness or un-happiness. It was the same for me.

At twenty-three, five years after my diagnosis, I still related my happiness to my weight. If I stepped on the scales and realized that I had lost weight, or if I peered into the mirror and noticed that my face was more drawn, and that my size ten jeans were slightly too baggy, I was still strangely filled with that same sense of delirium that triggered my descent into anorexia in the first place. Losing weight and gaining control were still capable of making me happy. As weight went up and down, moods followed suit. Feelings were in quick-shift mode.

I was, however, strong enough by this point to realize that one way out of my dependency on weighing scales was not to own any. I also decided it best to ignore them completely, not to even step on them, unless, on a very rare occasion, I needed to for some medical purpose (or maybe once in a while in a fit of desperation to check things were still in balance). This was a highly successful mechanism. Once I rejected them outright, they just gradually faded in importance. If I didn't have access to the anorexia-propelling information, I simply couldn't do anything about it. I didn't even have to consciously stop myself thinking about the scales because in the end something in my unconscious took over. Every time I remembered I wanted to weigh myself, I just as soon forgot. Perhaps it was because I had learned that the answers to my questions were never going to be resolved there.

Recovery, I think, is about growth in different ways, and for me it was about accepting womanhood, responsibility and change. The hardest thing here is to remove yourself from the pressure of normal expectation. Around us, the shape of the body seems to be the most important thing a woman can control. If the women that you are looking up to look like girls – in body, in shape and in essence – then it is hard to think that something different is right for you.

As an anorexic, you don't have a sense of what your 'self' equals, and so you think that if you can emulate others, something will form around you. If the images you are presented with are long and thin and glossy, it is easier to think you should be like that; it is easier to think that that is how and why those people have got there. You look up to them (models, celebrities, other thinner and seemingly happier people) and think that you will be made by your thinness. You can begin to believe that your success will be built from it, and that your self-esteem will somehow emerge from a thinner body.

I wonder how we have ended up here. How we ended up using the control and choice we now have as women to fight this battle. There are just too many expectations, conflicting ones, which can't be forged on one body; it cannot split so many ways and achieve them all perfectly. These expectations have been internalized and they have split us apart.

For so long, I didn't know who I was, and which of these expectations to follow. All I could think was that if I presented myself as thin and attractive then that's what people would take out of meeting me. That's what they would say: 'Grace – yes, that slim, thin girl.'

I liked that. That was a good way to describe me, and it was a good way to think of myself. Then it made it so much easier to take the bad bits (possible failure and criticism). But looking ahead and behind me for the first time, I realized that I had to be more.

It is hard to accept that you have to find your own level, which is inevitably a different level from everyone else's. It's hard to stop staring, to pull away, to stop wishing for a transformation to someone else's idea of 'the right shape'. Your inside strength finds it hard to come through, but when it does, you stop the self-rejection. You start to think of yourself as your own unique shape, your own outline.

Almost simultaneously, once I started to think of myself in my own shape, away from the expectations of others, a grown-up, out-grown anorexia me, I found myself stuck with the question in my head at all moments when I was alone: *'How do you feel?'* (That dreaded question!) *'Are you OK?'*

I could at first hear this voice, and then it was my voice, and I owned it. I didn't preempt it, I didn't forcibly ask myself. It seemed to come from within me, like a sense check, to make me take a step back, to make me assess myself in the moment. To make me sit with myself in the present and feel things. Feel my body; help me listen to my state of mind. It was a hard thing to do. Perhaps it was my body protecting itself against pain. Like the reflex action of the hand against a burning stove, it protected me from any self-destructive intentions, it got in there first. It irritated me into talking back, and I could tell by the sound of my breath, by the clench of my teeth or by the tightness of my shoulders, how I was feeling, and I could start to answer, slowly.

PART 7

Finding My Shape

Twenty-five

I am twenty-four. I have decided to leave my advertising job. I bumped into it at the right time, but now things are different and I have to face my fears and try something I really want to do at this moment, and for myself. It has been hard figuring out exactly what that is because the anorexia manipulated a lot of my desires.

My dad always says to me, 'Nobody has willpower like you.'

He is right. Above any kind of pain I will shift things to make them right. I lost weight because I wanted to be thin and happy. I wanted some time out of the pressure, to try and sort myself out. Then I put weight back on because I decided it was time that I moved away and escaped. Then I hid things, because I wanted a fresh start. Since then, I have started again and again, so that no one would know the horrible, disastrous old me. Recently, I let some things slip because I felt like I wanted someone to give me some direction. Now I want to change things again. This is a different kind of change, and one that has been building slowly. It is a change that will not be aggressive or forced; it will be one which I will embrace and sit with and take my time over.

Enough. Enough.

I want to be twenty-four years old, and beyond this old version of myself. I go to speak to my manager to tell him that I am leaving. He tries to get me to stay, he gives me time, people to speak to; surely I can't be serious? But of course I am, I have decided, and he will not sway me. I smile.

If only he knew!

It is strange not having to get up and go to my proper job every day. It is different spending the days alone. But now the anorexia has moved away, it is easier to do. I have got my boyfriend, we live together and we support each other. It really doesn't seem necessary to restrict myself any more. Things are slower and quieter and I don't feel the need to run anywhere. I need to momentarily step back, instead of charging on to the next thing to achieve. A bigger achievement will be to heal myself.

I sit on my sofa. I sit with my cup of tea and my chocolate biscuit and I start to think about my story and how I got here. I start to tell my story to myself. Now I am at home, in my London flat, on my own. Thinking things through, slowly, like I have never been able to do. I get up from the sofa and pace around the room. The jumping, thumping voices seem to calm down. I start with a line in my head. I think it might be a good way to start a novel about a girl with a big secret, one which she has sat on for years and years. I repeat a line to myself:

'If I share a secret with you, do you promise to tell everyone?'

The words spin round and round in my head. I sit at my desk and I start to tell this story. Hours have passed and I have forgotten all about going to the gym. I meant to go at three o'clock and now it is six, and actually I am quite hungry. It wasn't the story I thought I would write, but this one seems like the right one to tell, to begin with. There is a reason for it being told and a reason for it being read. There are things beyond me, things that I think will make sense for other people. It is not an inside story any more. It is the sort of story I wish I could have read; a story close to home. I decide to make myself some dinner. I eat it and I move on. I breathe out loud. Calm breathing. I start to climb in and out of my memories. They are really hard to find. The story of the girl is the story of this girl.

'In her story lies her survival.'

Yes, I think to myself, I think it does.

I balance on the edge of the pavement as a giggle of school-girls in grey uniform runs past me eating hot pizza. Laughing loudly, screaming. Was I? Am I? I can't quite decipher. I imagine the taste of melted cheese on top of red ripe toma-toes on top of hot, sticky dough. I haven't thought about that for years – what I was like before. Who was I? Who would I have been, right now? I have just lived through every day and moved on. I haven't dared look back. I stare at the girls in the grey school uniform and I think about when I was at school. Standing in line for my lunch at the canteen eating egg mayonnaise sandwiches in white bread for lunch followed by chocolate crispy cake, washed down with a carton of creamy milk. I see myself sitting and laugh-ing with my friends, my multitude of best friends. We are talking about our adventures on Friday night, about boyfriends, about universities, about almost being eighteen. About the freedom and the excitement it will bring us. About being proper grown-ups. We play with our hair and we put on our lip gloss and we saunter through the school, in charge of the corridor, on the edge of a new world:

'I'm Grace Bowman. I am eighteen. I am on the edge of a shape at the moment. I have just finished my A levels. I'm going to go to university and I'm going to study drama. I have got a boyfriend but that probably won't work out because I think I will want to be independent when I go to university and meet lots of new people. I enjoy going out, dressing up in my high heels and dancing until it's morning. I have four best friends and we do everything together. We are all eighteen and we'll be friends for ever. I can't wait to get away and travel around the world and see lots of new and different and exciting places. I don't want to stay in one place all my life, like I have, in the same house. I have loads of ideas about what I might do when I finish university. I can't wait to see what will happen.'

I've just taken off my school uniform for the last time. I choose an outfit to wear, a new outfit to try on, to represent me.

I kneel down by the shore of the frosty North Sea. I smile at the camera, with sand in my hands and grains falling through the cracks between my fingers. The sea stretches out behind me – endless miles of gentle blue water. I stand up, turn around and dip my toes in. I step back and look at the ocean: cold, soft, lapping. I do not concentrate on the feeling of my toenail, my toe, my foot or my leg, and how cold and wet they are; instead I look outwards. I step back. I glance across the surface.

I am sitting in my house, the house in which I grew up. I am eating dinner with my mum. I am sipping a glass of white wine and eating a pizza. I spent a long time trying to escape from this. There must be so much more, I thought to myself. There is something bigger, something I need to see. Now I am looking back out over the fields from the bay window of the house watching these plots in the distance, marking out unvisited areas, new imaginings. I don't feel the same about it any more, not now I live in the bigger place (the place I had only been able to imagine in my head); not now I have seen what it was impossible to see from where I grew up.

★

After some time out, it feels easier to go back to a new job, something a bit more thought through. I am twenty-five. It is six years since the worst year. I am different today, no question. The anorexic version of me is a part of my memory, but she doesn't feel like she needs to be a part of my present. It is amazing now, but I am able to stop myself thinking about the fat on my stomach, or the depth and width of my thighs. One day like that came along, and then it was two days, and then three in a row. Imagine that! Three days in a row with hardly any fat feelings and a head focused on other things. Even better, sometimes I can't remember what I ate two days ago. Mostly I still remember today, but I certainly can't list everything over the last week. I can't even tell you the calorie content of a pizza, or a slice of toast with butter, or a can of Coke. In fact, it's almost as if I have been brainwashed not to remember – by my own brain. It's like I hypnotized myself backwards. Quite often I forget about my body and my weight, I stop thinking about it. I wonder if it is because I don't need to focus on that any more. In the same way that I don't remember everything I learned at school (quadratic equations or cumulative frequency). It's almost there. The sounds of the words aren't unfamiliar. I close my eyes and think hard to find them, but I don't really need to. I don't need them. Like I don't need to know the fat content of each type of biscuit on the shelves of Tesco.

The voice, the wrong-speed inside voice, has slowly faded. It is more like a whisper than a roaring shout. Sometimes I faintly hear it trying to come back. Sometimes I punch it out in the gym. Sometimes I breathe it away. Sometimes I sleep through it. Sometimes I laugh so loud that it disappears entirely. Sometimes I jump on my bed and do forward rolls; anything to mix it up, screw it right up, throw it out of the window.

I know every tick, movement and pulse from inside me. I know the limits and edges of my shape. I know every line I have etched upon myself and every inch of my skin. I did not want to know this before. I hid it under the baggy clothes. I feel it now. It's strange because I am feeling something I used to hate. It is not so unbearable after all. I have come to terms with it, with me. I feel like I am almost inside a grown-up version of what I left behind – so suddenly, so cruelly – at eighteen going on nineteen.

At the start of a new me.

My Story

Anorexia just lost its appeal – frankly, the view of thin me equals happy me was not fulfilling, nor truthful, nor logical. The equation didn't make sense. I had been reciting the same lines over and over again, and years later, the thinness had contributed nothing to my self-esteem (that had to come from somewhere else). It took me time to work this out. It took me time to outgrow it, until one day, or one series of days, I decided to stop running away from finishing it.

I decided to write about it not only because it needed an ending, but also because it left me with a feeling that what I had experienced was confusing, alienating and too painful to ever look at again. Perhaps that is why so many people cannot go back over it, and instead see it as a phase which happened to them, and which they can't fully explain. I don't feel satisfied with such a conclusion. I wanted to understand it so that I, and others, might have some insight into where anorexia starts from, and how it is possible to move beyond it. I know that other people have told a similar story from the outside of the illness (as a parent or a friend) or from right inside it where the voice of the illness is a powerful manipulator of the truth, but I wanted to do both. The first, reflective, outside angle gives context but, coming from so far away, it can only repeat tired explanations and curiously observe something from the edge. The inside view can be a dangerous one which leaps off the page and seems to shout proudly about its power. Other anorexics might be triggered by it being let loose in such a way – even though that is not its intention. It needs the reflection to temper it, to show it where it went wrong, to allow it to sit against something more removed from its self-absorption.

I really struggled at first to feel my story; my history. I thought it would be easy to slide back into my story because I owned it, but instead I could only see the edges of many stories, and many voices, and none of them felt like they were mine. I was not even sure if I wanted to acknowledge them as mine either. Who would want to admit such falli-bility, such self-destruction? I thought to myself. And who would want to put that into writing? This is what an eating disorder does; time after time it pushes you outside your-self, firstly so that you can survive it, and secondly as an act of disengagement because it is all too painful to admit.

Indeed, I believed that my story involved a folded-up, shameful, forgettable series of memories. The very nature of an eating disorder (the hiding of a problem, the em-barrassment and guilt felt at having a seemingly illogical addiction, the feeling that you and it are rejected because you and it are hopelessly misunderstood) makes it into the most secret of secrets.

The only way to really start to explain my experience was to step out of my memories. I had to take a look at my story from the outside. I looked down and I floated above it. I had this bird's eye view of myself, which resembled one of those pictures of a small house in a long street in a big town taken from the air. It was like getting a view of myself from the sky. If I couldn't be my own subject then I would be an object, one which I could pull apart and deconstruct and piece back together again from afar. To be honest, at first it was easier to do it like that, because then I didn't have to admit myself to it. The object of me could be many shapes and sizes and it could be all the things that I did not want to represent. I could escape my own involvement. Only when I had really thought about where I had come from, instead of trying to deny my very origins, could I then step back into my story. Instead of thinking that wiping out my experiences would be the way to go forward, instead of shamefully disguising my subject under some kind of fiction, I had to admit the joins in me. I had to admit that I am one long continuation and not a thousand 'selves'.

I had never let myself go backwards. I had looked over my shoulder and thrown the bad bits of me away. I had fudged stories of things that didn't happen to cover up the gaps. When I thought of the starved, alien me, I thought of a girl on a stage, or in a place I had imagined but had never really been to. I thought of myself as a character in a book, not like this one, but in a strange fairy tale. I would then look at her and comment, and observe and watch her. I could have kept on watching her but I would have never admitted my own part in things. So there came a point when I had moved so far past her, that I was able to see that I should not be ashamed of her. I should not be ashamed of me. I had to try and explain what had happened to me, not only for myself, but also for other people. I felt that I had lived through an experience that could shed light for others.

When you decide to allow yourself access to the reality of your eating disorder, past or present, that's when you empower it with an existence outside the confines it has shrouded itself in. That is when it can start to break down. When it is shared it is broken. The anorexia itself tries to stop such an invasion of its privacy, of course. It tries to stop any sense of an ending to keep its power within, and you have to fight this. You have to break the secrecy. In my *story* came my survival, not because it was cathartic, but because it showed I had an interest in something beyond my relationship with food. I was motivated again, I had a passion for something – writing – and I realized I was able to locate a sense of myself from this, instead of from the empty hollow I had been living in.

In order to share my story, I realized that I really did have to think about how to start it. I had to go back to the beginning. I didn't want to do this because I didn't want my anorexia to have anything to do with where I came from or be a part of any kind of unintentional legacy passed on to me. I wanted it to be a boxed up, separate part of my life. But a beginning, and my beginning, were necessary. I decided to look back, to involve myself in where I had come from (my family and my childhood), rather than running from it. I thought of my gran.

My gran told me that no two persons' knitting is ever the same, so if you leave your knitting half done, and someone else picks it up and starts their bit, you can see the join. One person knits tightly, the other loosely, so that the knitting becomes uneven; some parts are bound together with an almost concrete force, and others are sagging and holey. My knitting was pretty uptight and there were noticeable mistakes where I dropped a stitch and left a gaping hole. Mostly, I just never got round to finishing anything – it all became too big and too unimaginable. I could never visualize the finished article. I had other places to go and other ideas to start, or maybe it was just that finishing anything might mean that I would be judged and criticized, and I couldn't cope with the aftermath of that. I was too fragile, too protected. I couldn't cope with the possible rejection. Unlike my gran. Her sewing was always complete. Her work was finished and whole. It reflected her dedication and her skill. She would sit for hours with the needles between her hands and move the wool gently and thoroughly through them. My memory of her starts with her sturdy hands, which resisted the prick of a needle. Her skin was tough – it would not break. She passed the fabric down the line.

But our family fabric is incomplete – there are holes in people's memories and in our history. There are shades and colours of supposed memories, fragments of experiences and washed-out traces of lives. But mostly the family history is missing. In big chunks. Big, bulky chunks. Too big to begin with, or to end with. To break through the mystery would be like trying to cough up a whale. History has been veiled with a sheet of silence.

Two people will begin to try to talk through it and two people will begin to shake, their voices vibrating with the fear of uncovering and discovering as they start to pull apart the layers that shroud the memories; memories which are only ever thought, believed or supposed. The fear – of the pain, of the effort, of the unpicking of all of those stitches, which hold it all together – is absolute. And in my own seamed-up memories there has been such thickness that occasional shafts of light threw me into fear of who I am, what I am and what I could have been – so much so that each of my memories became self-sealing. In the silence of memory, and in the avoidance of any conflict or discussion around it, there was a sense that the surface of everything was perfect, closed and quiet. Perhaps it was the perfection which filmed my exterior that caused me to nurture such high ideals. Such way-too-high ideals.

Searching through and talking about my emotions was no more than the psychiatrists wanted to do, of course, but I couldn't, and didn't want to, tell them. At that time, they would have started telling me my own story back; they would have made me into this character in their own version of events. I was determined that this was my story, and I wanted to share it. In the sharing of it, perhaps I could also transform the view of it for other people, perhaps it might be seen as something understandable, or at least be seen with a new perspective, framed in a different way. I know that it is easier to rationalize it now. To sit here, pen in hand, working it through in many different ways, but at the time it made no sense at all. There was no space to make sense of it. All of us caught up in it were held suspended over time, but I also know that many people around me would have given anything for some illumination on what I was going through.

I wonder what my anorexic self would think of me disinheriting her power. She might reject it as not at all relevant; she might be angry that she was exposed, and that people outside of her control would have a better idea of how she was operating; she might even look for tips on how to starve herself better. She might just look at this story and make hers work even more viciously; further planning, further competition, further starving. I would have to hope that she would see more than this, and that in the end she would see the possibility for change and start to do something about it, that something would have caught her eye and helped her to see how to change, even if she initially felt it triggering her. Because beneath the layers of bravado, deep down, I know she is scared. She has no idea where she is going to end up but other people, those around her, they do, and they can begin to give her some direction, if she would only give them the chance. Perhaps this is a hope too far.

My story is not as extreme as others. I did not spend time as an inpatient in hospital; I did not deteriorate again and again; I did not experience all the possible stages of my illness. I do not tick every box. I am just in the middle of things. I had this part of my life, which moved things in a certain way and moved me with them. I was at a very low weight for only a matter of months and yet the residue of it lasted for years. It was a place I was in, a frame of mind, a situation, which changed me.

You see, I imagine that this story – this part of my life – may well not be something that I will want to write about when I am older, when the growing-up part of life might even be seen as insignificant, or childish, or even foolish, and when there may well be so many more important life lessons than the ones between teenager and young adult. Perhaps? Now I think it is important. It is not about me any more, it is about the world I have experienced, it is about the shapes expected of us, and the shapes we have chosen to make.

My gran would be proud of my story. Behind the strength of her hands and her seamless fabrics there were many tears ready to fall. Things that were never said. There was such unbroken silence, that to speak out loud was to create an explosion in the air. Nobody was ready for that. They would, instead, sit with their hands over their ears and hope that by the time they took their hands away the noise would have stopped. Then further silence and cups of tea. Instead, I have been digging in my back garden for broken pieces of pottery, scrambling through the dirt with my fingernails to discover old footpaths hidden beneath the dry soil. Like I did when I was a little girl, before things got too deep to dig for. And I have broken a secret because of this. There can no longer be a perfect silence in my house.

My Shape

It took me time to realize that my problems were not marginal, it took me time to realize that what I went through was not as obscure as people had made out. I stood back and started watching other people. I realized that my symptoms were just reflecting what a lot of people were doing at different levels, but somehow I had taken it too far, I had stepped over the boundary line. In a sense it was a good thing that I went too far, because what I was feeling was acknowledged and recognized and I got some help. I was watched, which I hated, but needed. At least I was stopped at a relatively early stage. I did not go as far as could have been possible. I was made aware that my problem needed attention, unlike the voices I hear of people who make themselves sick 'once in a while', or don't eat for a couple of weeks 'here and there', or those who binge and then starve, but who 'get on with life'. These are the people who don't make it to the categorization stage, who don't get the 'anorexic' or 'bulimic' or 'overeater' label, but who slide between controlled and uncontrolled and feel it is acceptable to do so. And they feel this because it is condoned, not only by outside forces, but from within us, from within our female communities. We take pride in our dieting achievement; we admire and are jealous of our friends' self-control. We binge-drink and eat fast food and then force ourselves into the gym for gruelling workouts – punishing ourselves for the wrongs of the night before. It seems that we have lost sight of why we are doing this; we seem to have stopped questioning it. And that is how, I think, anorexia and bingeing have slid into society's vocabulary as if they are just an adjunct to our regular, everyday, self-imposed body and food restrictions. It is a dangerous path we are taking.

People ask me what they could have done to make things better, or what they can do now to stop it happening to someone else, to stop it taking hold even further than it has. I tell them that there is no simple formula. I tell them my story, because it is all I know how to tell. I tell them that as I was drowning in my own desperate bid for control, people sent me many a life-jacket and multiple rescue boats. People sat, swam, sunk in the water with me, even when I told them to go away. They even tried standing on the shore, keeping their distance (because they had given up on the other routes), while they watched me try and drown myself, even though it was the most painful thing for them to do. I wish I had the 'right' answer. In the end I had to help myself. I had to learn to grow out of it. I had to step outside it. I had to leave it, leaving me to feel absent, really horribly so. I had to be brave and face my fears and grow up in my own time, in my own shape. I had to help myself, but always with the continual and unending help, support and love of others. As much as I liked to think it, I did not get better on my own.

I have revealed my secret, beginning to end. I will not change my name, or run from it, or disguise it in an act of shame. It is ten years now since I was eighteen; since I felt like going on a diet, since I first discovered my fear of growing up; since my life was taken over by anorexia nervosa. I needed some time away from the force of the emotions and decisions that hit me in adolescence. I needed some space within myself and I found it through this illness. I found a place to hide away. An act of defence turned into one of attack, upon myself. I wasn't used to emotions, I was more of a thinker than a feeling person; I didn't know what to do. That is just the type of girl I was, and is still some of the woman that I am. It is not all down to personality, of course, but it is hard when you are like that, when you are on the inside most of the time, in your own imagination, full of fear, full of infinite possibility. It is hard to become more outside, a little more open, a little less enclosed.

Ten years on, and I made it through university, through first, second, third job, the twists and turns of the early twenties. Happiness and contentment within myself have come with hard work over a long time. They have come with the love of my fiancé, with growing self-belief and with others' belief in me.

I don't want to be everything any more. I don't want to be the successful power woman, the gym-obsessed, super-controlled machine, who suddenly has to transform into a lover, and then mother, and at the same time look like the svelte shadow of a girl. I would rather have balance; I would rather be less of these things, and feel a little more of my life.

The first thing people do when I tell them I once had anorexia is that they look me up and down. (I am a small person. If I had never been anorexic, I wonder if I would have ended up in this shape anyway. Without all of those attempts at self-moulding, I think I would.) Of course, I understand why; I cannot stop their interest. For my part, I have stopped thinking about my body so much, and I have accepted that it will change as I change, and as I grow older. So what I weigh today, or yesterday, or tomorrow will not tell you anything about me. It will not tell you who I am, what kind of person I am, what I believe or what I will be tomorrow.

I try and keep a balance, and that is my way. Sometimes this means taking a step back and away from the noise and the pressure around me. And sometimes it means relinquishing my control and letting other people run my day for me. This is important. To give up some control you need to give yourself and your time to someone else's plans, to someone else's needs; to do things for other people. This helps to break through the fear of what will happen if your life isn't planned just the way you want it to be. You can't control everything, and never will, and once you have accepted this you begin to steady.

I used to feel an absence from myself. I discarded my body, I threatened it, I tried to shrink it. Now I feel it, I sit in the presence of myself and I nurture it. It has helped to try and link my body and my mind, rather than separating them out and letting them fight each other. I feel like I am not fighting myself any more.

I actually feel protective of my body now. This is my shape, my body. This is my shape, my life.

A Letter

I feel like I am on the edge of your story but I don't feel like I am ready to admit it, so please don't tell anyone. I don't think that things are that bad. I'm not drowning, no, not at all. In fact, I have never been a better swimmer, but I know that if I stop swimming, even for a second, then I am not sure what will happen. It is the only way I know how to cope with things, so I just keep moving on, and I do look around sometimes at what I was before, and I think it would be a good idea to go back, but I don't know how. Not now I have started. I have tried to sort it out and I have sort of got it back under control again but every time I do, something else reminds me why I started in the first place. And this cannot be a public thing, so please don't tell anyone. I shouldn't have mentioned it, should I?

Anon.

I wish I could swim out to find you, and that you would listen to me, and that we could both come back to shore together. This is what I wish. But I think that if I came near, you would only swim out further, in a panic, fearing that I might make you do something that you are not ready to do. I can only show and tell you my own story from afar, hold it up for you, and hope that you might not have got so deep into things, that you may just be able to pull yourself out. I have been sharing my story so that if you want, you can listen, and you can maybe try to reach out your hand for some kind of a float. There are so many things I would like to say to you, but even I would not know where to start. I feel that I should be able to better explain it, but that is the agony of this thing; it sort of seizes you up and freezes you out. Can you feel that? That is why we talk in metaphors because we don't want to admit to the reality of it. And we feel that it is easier that way, don't we?

So instead I have made this story of my real and honest memories; more honest than I thought possible. Things are living in vivid, out-loud colours. Secrets from below the surface are on display. Maybe something will make sense for you, and you will start to see how things can change. There are ways out. There are endings. You don't have to sit with it for years. But you can't do it all on your own, sometimes you need someone to help. All you need to do to start off with is to put out your hand and ask for some-one else's. Don't drown. Fight it. Come with me to

The End.

Notes

1 Prevalence figures for eating disorders in the UK (diagnosed and undiagnosed): 1.15 million people, Eating Disorders Association [EDA] website www.edauk.com (27 August 2004, Norwich, UK).

2 'Doctors say sufferers are attention seekers'. An article on the findings of the EDA research, 'Getting Better? Is the quality of treatment for eating disorders in the UK getting better?' *Observer* (6 February 2005).

3 Diagnostic criteria for eating disorders, American Psychiatric Association (Diagnostic and Statistical Manual, DSM IV, 1994).

4 'The most commonly used proxy is 10 per cent of all cases of eating disorders will be male' (EDA, 2000), EDA website www.edauk.com (27 August 2004).

5 'The average age of onset for anorexia nervosa has been reported to be between 16.6 and 18.3 years', Theander, 1970; Halmi, 1974; Crisp et al. (1980), EDA www.edauk.com (27 August 2004).

6 Article in the *Daily Telegraph*, 8 March 2005, quoting Dr Andrew Hill, Senior Lecturer in Behavioural Sciences at Leeds University Medical School.

7 A. H. Crisp, *Anorexia Nervosa: Let Me Be*, Psychology Press, 1995.

8 Susan Willard, NOVA/Transcripts: 'Dying to be thin', www.pbs.org/wgbh/nova/transcripts/2715thin.html, (WGBH Educational Foundation and Twin Cities Public Television, 2000).

9 Forty-two per cent of GPs did not make an early diagnosis, 'Getting Better? Is the quality of treatment for eating disorders in the UK getting better?', EDA (7 February 2005).

10 Fifty-five per cent of people are not being treated by a specialist, 'Getting Better? Is the quality of treatment for eating disorders in the UK getting better?', EDA (7 February 2005).

11 Anorexia nervosa has one of the highest rates of mortality for any psychiatric condition: 13–20 per cent per annum, Howlett et al. (1995), EDA website www.edauk.com (27 August 2004).

12 P. F. Sullivan, 'Mortality in anorexia nervosa', *American Journal of Psychiatry* (1995), 152 (7), 1073–4. Cited in 'In-Patient Versus Out-Patient Care For Eating Disorders – A West Midlands Development and Evaluation Service Report' (Development and Evaluation Service, Department of Public Health and Epidemiology, University of Birmingham, 1999).

13 A. H. Crisp, *Anorexia Nervosa: Let Me Be.*

14 'Hilde Bruch argued that anorexia nervosa is caused by the failure to develop a diverse set of identities and self-definitions', Karen Farchaus Stein, PhD, RN and Linda Nyquist, PhD, 'Disturbance in the Self: A Source of Eating Disorders', article from *Eating Disorders Review* (January/February 2001), vol. 12, no.1 (Gurze Books, 2001).

15 'Disturbance in the Self: A Source of Eating Disorders', Karen Farchaus Stein, PhD, RN and Linda Nyquist, PhD, article from *Eating Disorders Review* (January/February 2001), vol. 12, no. 1 (Gurze Books, 2001).

16 'Family studies have shown the prevalence of eating disorders is 7 to 12 times higher among relatives of anorexic or bulimic probands than among controls', 'Serotonin: Implications for the Etiology and Treatment of Eating Disorders', Walter H. Kaye and Michael Strober, PhD, *Eating Disorders Review*, vol. 10, no. 3. (May/June 1999).

17 Walter Vandereycken and Ron Van Deth, *From Fasting Saints to Anorexic Girls: The History of Self-Starvation*, p. 4, (The Athlone Press, 1994).

18 Yogarexia, reported in the *Guardian* Weekend (26 February 2005).

19 David Knight and Steven Bratman, *Health Food Junkies*: The *Rise of Orthorexia Nervosa – The Health Food Eating Disorder* (Broadway Books, 2001).

20 Stressorexia, reported in the *Independent on Sunday* (5 December 2004).

21 'Whilst the incidence of anorexia nervosa appears to have remained fairly constant over time, that of bulimia nervosa appears to be increasing rapidly. Turnbull et al. (1996) have suggested a fivefold increase in the incidence of bulimia nervosa over a five-year period from 1988 to 1993', EDA website www.edauk.com (27 August 2004).

22 Richard Morton's *Phthisiologia; or, a Treatise of Consumptions* (translated from the original 1689 Latin edn, London, 1694), in which he describes 'Atrophia nervosa': to waste away from nervous consumption.

23 *The New Shorter Oxford English Dictionary*.

24 Dr Ernest Charles Lasègue, 'On Hysterical Anorexia', translated from *Archives Générales de Médecine* (April 1873), *The Medical Times and Gazette*, 2, (London, 1973). Quoted in *From Fasting Saints to Anorexic Girls: The History of Self-Starvation*, Walter Vandereycken and Ron Van Deth, p. 157 (The Athlone Press, 1994).

25 *Anorexia Nervosa: Let Me Be*, A. H. Crisp.

26 Charlotte Brontë, *Shirley*, World Classics, 1991.

27 'One in every 250 females experiences anorexia in adolescence and young adulthood, and five times that number suffer from bulimia', National Institute for Clinical Excellence (2004). Eating Disorders. NICE Clinical Guideline No. 9, London, National Institute for Clinical Excellence. Available from www.nice.org.uk.

28 Russell, 1979: Fairburn and Cooper, 1984, Mitchell et al. 1986, EDA website www.edauk.com (14 November 2004).

29 'Bulimia Nervosa was not recognized as a clinical condition until Gerald Russell's paper, published in the UK in

1979', EDA website www.edauk.com (27 August 2004).

30 'Eating disorders can persist throughout life and people may fluctuate between anorexia and bulimia nervosa', EDA website www.edauk.com (27 August 2004).

31 Diagnostic criteria for eating disorders, American Psychiatric Association (Diagnostic and Statistical Manual, DSM IV, 1994).

32 A. H. Crisp, *Anorexia Nervosa: Let Me Be*, p. 33.

Recommended Reading

When I was anorexic, I really liked reading about anorexia. Unfortunately, it was often for the wrong reasons, and encouraged my disordered behaviour. As I began to recover, however, I found inspiration and guidance within those same words, which I hadn't been able to see before. The very fact that my illness was being discussed and analysed helped me to see beyond myself. I believe that all the books I have listed here have clearly good intentions behind them. They offer practical advice, useful information or personal or historical viewpoints on the illness for the benefit of others.

Personal stories

Chisholm, Kate, *Hungry Hell*, Short Books, 2002.
    A clear and concise account of the author's own experience of anorexia, balanced out with informative historical and theoretical sources.

Hornbacher, Marya, *Wasted*, Flamingo, 1998.
    American writer's brutally honest memoir of her experience of eating disorders. Her powerfully punchy writing engulfs the reader into the very extremes of her illness. This is a no-holds-barred tale of her struggles, which had very severe effects.

Lindsay, Clare, *Conquering Anorexia: The Route to Recovery*, Summersdale, 2000.
    An accessible, simply written diary account of anorexia, and

the author's experience of differing treatments, including a useful section on self-help techniques and exercises for those looking for help with recovery strategies.

Self-help

Cooper, Peter, and Fairburn, Christopher, *Bulimia Nervosa and Binge-eating: A Guide to Recovery*, Constable & Robinson, 1993.

This guide is suitable for sufferers and their family and friends. It contains a wealth of information to aid understanding and discusses treatment options. Part Two of the book offers a self-help programme with effective strategies for beating the problem.

Crisp, Arthur, Joughin, Neil, Halek, Christine, and Bowyer, Carol, *Anorexia Nervosa: The Wish To Change*, Psychology Press (second edition), 1996.

Dr Crisp is a leading expert on anorexia. This book provides a step-by-step programme for change for those suffering from anorexia. It would be most effective for those already committed to trying to combat their anorexia, but unsure about how to start.

Fairburn, Christopher, *Overcoming Binge Eating*, Guilford Press, 1995.

Includes clear information about eating disorders and a comprehensive self-help guide for recovery from binge-eating disorders.

Freeman, Christopher, and Cooper, Peter, *Overcoming Anorexia Nervosa: A self-help guide using Cognitive Behavioural Techniques*, Constable & Robinson, 2001.

This is a complete self-help recovery programme to overcoming anorexia using cognitive therapy techniques.

Treasure, Janet, *Breaking Free From Anorexia Nervosa: A Survival Guide for Families, Friends and Sufferers*, Psychology Press, 1997.

This often recommended book aims to answer questions raised by the illness for a variety of readers. It includes an overview of anorexia, different perspectives on the illness, and reassurance and guidelines for professionals, patients and their families.

Fiction

Brontë, Charlotte, *Shirley*, Oxford World Classics, 1991.

Female starvation hinges on the line between power and powerlessness in this nineteenth-century novel.

Hamsun, Knut, *Hunger*, translated by Sverre Lyngstad, Rebel Inc., 1996.

A captivating, hugely original and sometimes disturbing novel written in 1890, *Hunger* is an interior monologue of a young male writer suffering from the extreme effects of starvation, desolation and loneliness.

Rosen, Jonathan, *Eve's Apple*, Granta, 1997.

Observed from the perspective of an anorexic's male partner, this novel offers intelligent insights into the nature of appetite and obsession.

Poetry

Duffy, Carol Ann, *Feminine Gospels*, Picador, 2002.

This compelling book of poetry focuses on various shapes and forms of female identity.

For professionals and parents/carers

Bruch, Hilde, *The Golden Cage: The Enigma of Anorexia Nervosa*, Harvard University Press, 1978.

This classic text from the 1970s still provides insight into the illness for patients, parents, mental health trainees and senior therapists alike. Bruch focuses on the pursuit of thinness and the formation of identity.

Crisp, Arthur, *Anorexia Nervosa: Let Me Be*, Psychology Press, 1995.

A clinical perspective on anorexia nervosa, Dr Crisp's focus is that of the development of the illness and the challenges posed by puberty and growth. This book is suited to those with a professional interest in the subject, or to parents or sufferers who value a more in-depth and detailed clinical approach.

Duker, Marilyn, and Slade, Roger, *Anorexia Nervosa & Bulimia: How to Help*, Open University Press, 1988.

This book is intended for helpers and carers of all kinds who are concerned with the best methods to help. Describes what that help can involve, drawing upon the authors' own experience with clients.

Lawrence, Marilyn, *The Anorexic Experience*, Women's Press Handbook, 2001(first edn 1984).

An informed perspective from a therapist at the Women's Therapy Centre, this is a clear and accessible guide to approaching the illness.

Related issues

Orbach, Susie, *On Eating*, Penguin, 2002.

A helpful guidebook from the author of *Fat is a Feminist Issue*, this little book offers tips and pointers on redressing your relationship with food and eating. The advice is clear, easy to digest and calming.

Schmidt, Ulrike, and Treasure, Janet, *Getting Better Bite by Bite: A Survival Kit for Sufferers of Bulimia Nervosa and Binge Eating Disorders*, Psychology Press, 1993.

A useful manual offering help to those with bulimia and binge-eating disorders. It provides suggestions for further reading as well as advice on a wide spectrum of relevant topics.

Wurtzel, Elizabeth, *Prozac Nation*, Quartet Books, 1995.

A powerful account of living with depression and self-harm embedded with an astute cultural awareness of America at the end of the twentieth century.

History/social context

Ellmann, Maud, *The Hunger Artists: Starving, Writing and Imprisonment*, Virago, 1993.

An academic perspective which provides a unique and original view, exploring self-starvation through themes of hunger, writing and imprisonment.

Jacobs Brumberg, Joan, *Fasting Girls: The History of Anorexia Nervosa*, Vintage, 2000.

An interesting analysis of the condition from a historical perspective.

Vandereycken, Walter, and Van Deth, Ron, *From Fasting Saints to Anorexic Girls: The History of Self-Starvation*, The Athlone Press, 1994.

A detailed international perspective on self-starvation over the centuries, with a particular focus on the relevance of the socio-cultural context.

Wolf, Naomi, *The Beauty Myth*, Vintage, 1991.

A highly charged, stat-packed book which still sparks debate about the way in which images and idealizations of female beauty are used to maintain the male-dominated power structures.

Woolf, Virginia, *A Room of One's Own*, Penguin Classics, 2000.

In this classic text, Woolf expresses the effects of poverty and social constraints on female creativity and intellectual freedom.

Directory of Useful Addresses

Anorexia Nervosa and Related Eating Disorders, Inc.
www.anred.com

American-based website containing information about anorexia nervosa, bulimia nervosa, binge-eating, compulsive exercising and other less well-known food and weight disorders, and includes statistics, warning signs, personal stories and links.

Body Whys
www.bodywhys.ie
PO BOX 105
Blackrock
Co Dublin
Ireland

Telephone helpline: 00 353 1 890 200 444 (Mondays, Wednesdays 7.30 p.m. to 9.30 p.m.; Tuesdays, Fridays 12.30 p.m. to 2.30 p.m.; Thursdays 10 a.m. to 12 noon)

Email: info@bodywhys.ie

Irish national charity offering help and support for people with eating disorders, their friends and families.

Careline
www.carelineuk.org
Cardinal Heenan Centre
326–328 High Road
Ilford
Essex IG1 1QP

Tel. 020 8514 1177 (Monday to Friday 10 a.m. to 1 p.m. and 7 p.m. to 10 p.m.)

Provides a confidential crisis telephone counselling service for children, young people and adults on any issue including eating disorders.

Centre for Eating Disorders (Scotland)
www.maryhart.co.uk
3 Sciennes Road
Edinburgh EH9 1LE
Tel. 0131 668 3051 (usually an answer-phone service)
Email: info@maryhart.co.uk

Offers psychotherapy and counselling aimed at helping to change eating habits and attitudes. Has a range of self-help manuals on types of eating disorders, causes, self-help, plus a publications list.

Eating Disorders Association (EDA)
www.edauk.com
103 Prince of Wales Road
Norwich NR1 1DW

Adult telephone helpline: 0845 634 1414 (weekdays 8.30 a.m. to 8.30 p.m., Saturdays 1 p.m. to 4.30 p.m.)

Helpline email: helpmail@edauk.com

Youthline telephone: 0845 634 7650 (weekdays 4 p.m. to 6.30 p.m., Saturdays 1 p.m to 4.30 p.m.)

Youthline email: talkback@edauk.com

Youthline TEXT service: 07977 493 345

Recorded message (10 minutes/50p per minute): 0906 302 0012

A national charity offering help and information to people with anorexia and bulimia nervosa, and their families and friends. Provides advice and publications on all aspects of eating disorders. Operates a UK-wide telephone helpline for people with an eating disorder, their family, friends, and professionals, along with a youthline that offers information, help and support for young people aged eighteen years and under.

Eating Disorders Resources
www.edr.org.uk

Information website with news, reports, research, conferences and opinions on eating disorders including anorexia nervosa, bulimia nervosa, compulsive eating and binge-eating, with details of organizations, publications and links to other websites.

First Steps to Freedom
www.first-steps.org
1 Taylor Close
Kenilworth
Warwickshire CV8 2LW
Telephone helpline: 0845 1202916 (10 a.m. to 10 p.m. daily)
General enquiries: 01926 864473
Email: first.steps@btconnect.com

Aims to help in a practical way people who suffer from phobias, obsessive compulsive disorders, anxiety, panic attacks, anorexia and bulimia. Provides a confidential helpline offering counselling, listening, advice, support and information.

The International Eating Disorders Centre
www.eatingdisorderscentre.co.uk
119–121 Wendover Road
Aylesbury
Bucks HP21 9LW
Tel. 01296 330557
Email: webenquiry@eatingdisorderscentre.co.uk

The centre provides multi-disciplinary rehabilitation programmes for eating disorder sufferers.

Mental Health Foundation

www.mentalhealth.org.uk
London Office:
9th Floor, Sea Containers House
20 Upper Ground
London SE1 9QB
Tel. 020 7803 1100 (Monday to Friday 10.30 a.m. to 4 p.m.)
Email: mhf@mhf.org.uk

Scotland Office:
Merchants House
30 George Square
Glasgow G2 1EG
Tel. 0141 572 0125
Email: scotland@mhf.org.uk

Offers information and literature on all aspects of mental health, including where to get help, information about specific mental health problems, treatments and rights.

The National Centre for Eating Disorders

www.eating-disorders.org.uk
54 New Road
Esher
Surrey KT10 9NU
Tel. 0845 838 2040

Provides information on eating disorders such as compulsive or binge-eating, anorexia, bulimia and dieting. Offers information, counselling and professional training.

NHS Direct

www.nhsdirect.nhs.uk
Tel. 0845 4647 (24-hour nurse advice and health information service)

Provides information and advice on all health topics.

National Institute for Clinical Excellence
www.nice.org.uk
MidCity Place
71 High Holborn
London WC1V 6NA
Tel. 020 7067 5800
Email: nice@nice.org.uk

Includes official eating disorder treatment guidelines.

Patient UK – Introduction to Anorexia
www.patient.co.uk/showdoc/23069106

Provides information leaflets, details of support groups and a directory of UK websites.

The Royal College of Psychiatrists
www.rcpsych.ac.uk/info/eatdis.htm

Provides information leaflets on eating disorders and links to useful organizations, books and reports.

Something Fishy Website on Eating Disorders
www.something-fishy.org

US pro-recovery website dedicated to raising awareness about eating disorders, providing support and information for those with eating disorders, and their family and friends.

Women's Therapy Centre
www.womenstherapycentre.co.uk
10 Manor Gardens
London N7 6JS
Tel. 020 7263 7860
Email: info@womenstherapycentre.co.uk

Provides individual and group psychotherapy for women of all ages. Themes explored include compulsive eating and bulimia.

Website contains information about the services and therapies available.

Young Minds

www.youngminds.org.uk

48–50 St John Street

Clerkenwell

London ECIM 4DG

Tel. 020 7336 8445

Parents' information line: 0800 018 2138 Mondays, Fridays 10 a.m. to 1 p.m.; Tuesdays, Wednesdays, Thursdays 1 p.m. to 4 p.m.; Wednesday evenings 6 p.m. to 8 p.m.

Email: enquiries@youngminds.org.uk

Provides information and advice on child mental health issues.